A SERIES OF
NEW TESTAMENT
STUDY GUIDES

PRISON LETTERS

HELPS FOR
READING AND UNDERSTANDING
THE MESSAGE

Bob Young

James Kay Publishing

Tulsa, Oklahoma

A Series of New Testament Study Guides
PRISON LETTERS
Helps for Reading and Understanding the Message
ISBN 978-1-943245-24-6

www.bobyoungresources.com

www.jameskaypublishing.com
e-mail: sales@jameskaypublishing.com

Table of Contents

Preface to the Series

A number of factors have converged in my life as influences on my method of Bible study and Bible teaching. My undergraduate training in Bible and biblical languages served as the foundation for my first twenty-five years of full-time preaching ministry. During those years, I took graduate courses from time to time to develop my skills and to help keep my preaching and ministry fresh.

When I decided to pursue graduate education seriously, I already loved teaching from an exegetical viewpoint while paying special attention to the historical-cultural context and the grammatical-syntactical features of the biblical text. I had seen how excited people become when they learn how to read and understand the Bible. I had seen the healthy way in which people respond to thoughtful efforts to explain and apply the message of the Bible. I had developed the habit of doing in-depth Bible study as a part of my sermon preparation process. For those reasons, in my graduate training I wanted to study and understand the dynamics of effective ministry with a focus on preaching. I wanted to integrate academic studies of the biblical text with practical applications to inform my teaching and preaching. Because I did graduate work while continuing my full-time work in ministry, I was blessed by have a laboratory where I could apply and test what I was learning.

My years of teaching and administration in Christian higher education coupled with involvement in the world of missions have made me even more aware of the need to view the text, insofar as possible, outside one's own social, cultural, experiential, and religious backgrounds. My Bible study, teaching and preaching today are influenced by my training and experience as I try to understand the biblical context, the historical-cultural context, and the literary context—vocabulary, genres, grammar, and syntax. I want to understand the original message of the author and the purpose of the text as first steps toward understanding the message of the text in today's world. I want to know what the text said and what it meant, so that I can know what it says and what it means today.

In recent years, I have observed a lessening interest in studying the Bible. I fear that more and more Christians do not enjoy studying the Bible and do make Bible reading and study a part of their regular routines. I often see study of books about the Bible substituted for study of the Bible. I am saddened when people tell me the Bible is not understandable for them, or that they struggle to read and make relevant applications. I want to help reignite interest in Bible study. I want to share my excitement as I read and study the dynamic, living text of Scripture. I want to help people read with understanding and excitement.

I believe many of us would like to have help in reading and understanding without having to wade through many of the details that are often included in Bible study resources. As I have prepared these study guides, I have constantly asked myself, "What would I want in a study guide to the biblical text?" I have been guided by this question, generally excluding technical details and academic questions, but periodically including such items because of their value in understanding and communicating the text. I have tried to provide helps for reaching and study while avoiding multitudes of exegetical questions. Above all, I have tried to provide a practical guide to put in clear relief what the text says as a first step toward valid interpretation of what the text means and how it should be applied in the world today.

I wrote these guides with multiple readers in mind. Preachers and Bible class teachers will find a fresh study of the text helpful; Christians in the pews with an interest in the message of the Bible will be helped by the textual jewels and the textual summaries that are included. These guides are not designed to replace your Bible but to help you read and understand your own personal Bible. May God bless you in your desire and your efforts to understand and apply his Word!

--Tulsa, Oklahoma
July, 2018

Introduction to the Series

The Purpose of These Guides

To describe the publications included in this series as "Bible study guides" says something about their intended purpose. As guides, these little books do not attempt to answer every question that may arise in your study of the biblical text. They are not commentaries in the strictest sense of the word. The focus of these guides is distinct.

I have as a primary goal to encourage you to do your own study of the Bible. This series of study guides is designed to assist the Bible student with preliminary and basic reading while providing some basic tools, and to suggest some study methods that will enrich your study and help you identify the message of the text—whether in a specific verse or paragraph, a larger context, or an entire book of the New Testament. A primary goal of these guides is to help you maintain a focus on the purpose and message of the original author. The message of the original writer should inform our understanding of the text and its application today. One should not think that the message and meaning of the text today would be significantly different than the message and meaning of the original document.

The title also says that these guides are "helps." I have tried to provide resources to guide and enrich your study, keeping the purpose of the original author in view. This desire has informed the content of these study guides. Many study guides exist and there is no need to write more books that basically have the same content. Generally, the information included in these guides is designed to help identify the purpose of the original author and the message of the Bible. In some passages, the information included in these guides will provide insights not readily available in other resources.

What Kinds of "Helps" Are Included in These Guides?

These study guides reflect how I organize and understand the text of the Bible, taking into account various factors such as syntax, grammar, and vocabulary. Along the way, I share some observations that may help clarify passages that are difficult to understand. I have not tried to comment or treat in detail on every passage where potential problems or differences in understanding exist. I have not noted every textual variant in the original text. At times, these notes may seem to be unnecessary comments on passages where the meaning is clear to the reader; that probably means I am trying to share insights to deepen understanding and appreciation of the text. In other passages, some may ask why I have not included more comments or explanation. Such is the individualized nature of Bible study. The overall goal of my comments is to maintain a focus on the original author's message and purpose for writing—the "what he said and what he meant" of the original author in the original context.

For each chapter, there is a "Content" section that usually includes a brief outline, followed by notes ("Study Helps") about the biblical text. The content sections of these guides, including how the text is divided and how paragraphs are described, are drawn from my own reading and analysis of the text and from a comparison of several translations. In only a very few cases does the outline provided in this guide vary from the majority opinion, and those cases are noted and the reasons given. In some chapters, there is an overview with introductory comments to help orient the student to the overall content and message of the chapter. In a few chapters, there are some additional introductory observations. For some chapters a paraphrased summary is included as part of the textual study or in a separate section after the study helps. As noted above, these Bible study guides are not intended to answer every question. In a few cases, I have addressed topics that are not treated in detail in other resources. Texts that are easily understood and matters that are customarily included in other resources are, for the most part, not treated in detail in these books.

A Useful Tool for Understanding the Message of the Bible

While the primary purpose of these guides is to assist in personal study of the biblical text, these guides will also serve the casual reader who wants to understand the basic message of Scripture. The guides are written in such a way that the reader can understand the general message of the text, along with some helpful details, simply by reading the guide. One might describe theses guides as a kind of "CliffsNotes" to the Bible, but they are intended as helps and should not be thought of as taking the place of Bible reading and Bible study.

How to Use This Bible Study Guide in Personal Bible Study

This guide is not intended to take the place of your own Bible reading and study but is intended to provide insights and suggestions as you read the Bible and to be a resource that will help you check your understanding. **You are encouraged to use this guide and your own Bible side by side.** Some sections of this guide may be difficult to understand unless one can compare the specific part of the text that is being described or explained.

No specific translation of the biblical text is included in this guide. Two goals influenced the decision not to include a translation of the biblical text. First, it is hoped that you will be encouraged to use your own study Bible. Second, these notes are designed to be helpful in biblical study regardless of the version the reader may prefer for personal Bible study.

My primary purpose is to make it easier for you the reader and student to read, analyze, and understand the text. Ultimately, you are responsible for your own interpretation of the Bible and you cannot simply follow what a favorite preacher or commentator says. Often the study notes for a chapter or subsection of a chapter are followed by a brief summary of the text, focusing on the message.

Five Steps for Bible Study. The suggested process for effectively using these Bible study guides involves five steps. First, you should read an introduction to the book of the Bible you wish to study. The introductions provided in these guides will serve well. They are for the most part briefer than normal and do not cover every detail. In this series of guides, sometimes one introduction is provided to cover multiple books, as in the case of the Thessalonian correspondence and the Pastoral Letters.

The second step in your study is to read through the book of the Bible you wish to study to understand the overall content. It will be helpful if this can be done at a single sitting.

The student facing time constraints may have time for only one reading, but multiple readings will reveal additional details of the book, providing you an opportunity to notice repeated words and phrases and to think about the message of the book, how the book develops its message, and how various parts of the book are connected. You will find help for your reading in the chapter outlines that are provided in these study guides.

Now you are ready to begin your study of individual chapters or sections. The process is simple: read a section of the text until you have a good understanding of it. This step is not an in-depth reading to resolve every question but is a general reading to understand the contents of the passage.

The fourth step is for you to write your own outline of the chapter or section, with paragraphing that reflects major thought patterns, divisions, and topics. In these study guides, each chapter has a section with suggested paragraphing based on a comparison of various translations. While it is possible to skip this step in which you do your own analysis and paragraphing and to move directly to the paragraphing provided in the study guide, taking the shortcut is not the recommended approach. You will benefit from taking the time and investing the energy to do this work in initial reading and understanding.

Finally, the study guides have a section of study helps that will help you read and understand the text and keep the intent of the original author in mind as you do more focused study. In many chapters, a final section that summarizes the message of the chapter is included.

Initial Reading and Paragraphing

In other articles and publications, I have explained the importance of preparatory reading and personal study of the biblical text. In the five-step process described above, initial reading and paragraphing occur in the second, third, and fourth steps. When the student carefully works through these steps, it becomes clear that the study is a "Bible" study and is not simply a process of reading more background information and commentary from another human author who is trying to explain the Bible. Although many students of the Bible jump immediately from reading an introduction to reading a commentary, it is important that the serious Bible student learn to read and study the Bible for herself or himself. Once the biblical text is familiar, I suggest the student think about the themes that can be identified and how to mark the paragraph divisions, based on the contents of the passage and the subjects treated. Once this work is complete, it is good to compare the resulting paragraphing with that of several versions, or with the outlines in the content sections of these guides.

A Note About Paragraphing

Paragraph divisions are the key to understanding and following the original author's message. Most modern translations are divided into paragraphs and provide a summary heading. Ideally, every paragraph has one central topic, truth, or thought. Often, there will be several ways to describe the subject of the paragraph. Only when we understand the original author's message by following his logic and presentation can we truly understand the Bible. Only the original author is inspired—readers must take care not to change or modify the message. A first step toward integrity with the text is to develop the ability to analyze it and establish paragraphs.

Note: This introductory information about personal Bible study, reading, and paragraphing is not repeated for each chapter. Students will find it helpful to return to this introductory section again and again to guide their study, especially before beginning the study of a new chapter of the Bible.

Resources

The Greek text used is the 27th edition of *Novum Testamentus Graece* which is identical with the 4th revised edition of *The Greek New Testament*. Other tools I find helpful include my Greek concordance (Moulton and Geden), Greek lexicons (Arndt and Gingrich, and some older lexicons), and Greek vocabulary studies (*Theological Dictionary of the New Testament*; *Dictionary of New Testament Theology*, Colin Brown; and Moulton and Milligan).

Several English translations have been consulted. Those consulted most frequently include the English Standard Version (ESV), New English Translation (NET), and New International Version (NIV).

Various commentaries and study tools have been consulted in preparing these study guides. The on-line studies by Utley reflect my own training and ideas about how to approach the biblical text. That I have studied his work may be apparent in my explanations of some texts.

A Few Other Matters

No footnotes are included in these Bible Study Guides. Comments that are often included in footnotes have been inserted parenthetically into the text. Since I have worked primarily from the biblical text, language tools, and my own notes, no bibliography is supplied.

I am grateful for the teachers and professors who taught me to love the text and helped me develop the skills that make the study of the Bible a rich experience. I want to thank those who have encouraged me to put my teaching style in written form. These study guides reflect much of what I would share in teaching a Bible class. For the most part, these written materials do not include the applications I would make of the text since applications must always be contextualized.

Finally, I am grateful to my wife, Jan, for her support and encouragement in this endeavor. Writing requires time, and the office time I have invested has meant less time spent with her.

A Word About Formatting

The format of the Study Helps in each chapter follows the outline that is provided for the chapter. The major points of the outline are used to begin new sections of the Study Helps. Biblical references that introduce sections or subsections of the Study Helps are placed in bold type to assist the student. In the case of paragraphs that cover multiple verses, the biblical references are placed in progressive order on the basis of the first verse in the citation.

Standard abbreviations of biblical books are used. Verse citations that do not include the name of a book (e.g. 2:14) refer to the book being studied. Abbreviations that may not be familiar to some readers include the following: cf. = compare; e.g. = for example; v. = verse; vv. = verses.

The first time a translation is mentioned, the standard abbreviation is included for translations that are less well-known. Subsequent references use only the abbreviation.

Greek words are placed in italics. Often, the corresponding Greek word, a literal meaning, and other translation possibilities are placed in parentheses immediately after an English word. Greek words are written as transliterations in English letters, using the basic lexical form of the word. It is hoped that this will make it easier for the reader without a working knowledge of Greek. Many readers will find these references interesting, especially in identifying those passages where there is repeated use of the same Greek word. Readers can quickly pass over this inserted parenthetical information if desired.

In a few cases, parentheses are used to indicate Greek verbal forms or noun forms where this information would be significant to the student with an understanding of grammar. The Greek language uses three classes of conditional statements: clauses that begin with "if." These constructions are noted when the use is significant. The first class condition is assumed to be true from the viewpoint of the author. The second class condition is contrary to fact. The third class condition is hypothetical. Again, the reader can pass over this information rapidly if desired.

The Greek text used is the 27th edition of *Novum Testamentus Graece* which is identical with the 4th revised edition of *The Greek New Testament*.

Quotation marks are often used to call attention to special words or topics, and also to indicate citations or translations of the biblical text, most of which are my own. This usage will help the reader identify references to the biblical text since no specific translation of the biblical text is included in this Study Guide.

Parentheses are used liberally to enclose information and comments that would often be included in footnotes. It is hoped that readers will find this more convenient, both those who want to read the expanded explanation and those who wish to skip over the parenthetical material.

Comments concerning contemporary applications of the text are limited since they do not reflect the primary purpose of these study helps. Nonetheless, observations about how the text is to be applied are included from time to time.

Summaries are provided for many chapters, with the goal of helping to make the message of the chapter clearer. Some of these summaries are paraphrases, some are written in first person, from the standpoint of the author; others are written in third person and are explanations of the message of the chapter. Summaries written in either the first person or third person are not translations and they are not paraphrases. They are attempts to communicate the basic points and the purpose of the original message.

Introduction to Ephesians

Ephesians has been called the "crowning jewel" of Paul's theology although the book is not primarily a theological treatise. Ephesians is typically Pauline, primarily written for teaching and application. The book follows Paul's normal pattern of pedagogical materials followed by practical applications.

Ephesians was popular among the Reformers. John Calvin called it his favorite book of the Bible and John Knox asked that Calvin's sermons on Ephesians be read to him when he was on his deathbed. The message of unity in Christ remains popular in the contemporary church.

Authorship, Date, and Recipients

<u>Author</u>. That Paul is the author is stated in 1:1 and 3:1, and is reflected in an almost unanimous opinion of church tradition. Clement of Rome cited Eph. 4:4-6 in A.D. 95, and Ignatius (d. A.D. 107) quoted from the book. Polycarp, Irenaeus, and Clement of Alexandria all asserted that Paul authored the book. Ephesians is among Paul's writings in the Muratorian Fragment. Paul's authorship has been questioned because of the lack of personal greetings, but this would be normal if the book was first written as a circular letter (see below concerning the recipients). The book contains very long sentences that are not characteristic of Paul's other writings, and has some unique vocabulary. However, the number of unique words (*hapax legomena*, a phrase that means "only written") in the book of Ephesians is the same as the number of unique words in the book of Romans. The purpose, subject matter, recipients and occasion easily explain the use of different words.

<u>Date</u>. The date of this letter is linked to one of Paul's imprisonments in Ephesus, Philippi, Caesarea, or Rome. A Roman imprisonment best fits the facts of Acts. The best educated guess for the writing of Ephesians is Paul's first imprisonment in Rome in the early 60s. Tychicus, along with

Onesimus, probably took the letters of Colossians, Ephesians and Philemon to Asia Minor.

Here is a likely chronology of Paul's writings, with approximate dates.

Book	Date	Place of Writing	Relationship to Acts
Galatians	50	Syrian Antioch	Acts 14:28; 15:2
1 Thessalonians	51	Corinth	Acts 18:5
2 Thessalonians	51	Corinth	Acts 18
1 Corinthians	55	Ephesus	Acts 19:20
2 Corinthians	56	Macedonia	Acts 20:2
Romans	57	Corinth	Acts 20:3
Colossians	early 60s	Rome	Acts 28
Philemon	early 60s	Rome	Acts 28
Ephesians	early 60s	Rome	Acts 28
Philippians	early 60s	Rome	Acts 28
1 Timothy	63 (or later)	Macedonia	
Titus	63 ??		
2 Timothy	64-68	Rome	

<u>Recipients</u>. The question of who were the recipients hinges on a textual question in 1:1. Some manuscripts (Chester Beatty Papyri, p^{46}; Sinaiticus, ℵ; Vaticanus, B; Origen's Greek text, and Tertullian's Greek text) omit "in Ephesus" in 1:1. This has led to the speculation that the letter may have originally been intended as a cyclical or circular letter. The Greek grammar of Eph. 1:1 can accommodate a place name. Perhaps the place name was left blank so it could be supplied when read aloud to the churches. This would explain the absence of personal greetings. Other manuscripts include the phrase "in Ephesus" and the name attached to the letter today reflects those manuscripts.

Beyond the textual question of 1:1, one can note that Ephesians was written to a church (or to churches) that had Gentiles among its members (2:1, 11; 4:17).

The Literary Relationship between Ephesians and Colossians

The literary relationship between Ephesians and Colossians is best understood against the backdrop of the historical relationship between Colossians and Ephesians.

Epaphras (Col. 1:7; 4:12; Philemon 23) was apparently converted during Paul's Ephesian ministry (Acts 19).

He may have been instrumental in starting three churches--in Hierapolis, Laodicea and Colossae. When difficulties arose in the Colossian church (relating to the emerging desire to integrate Christianity, philosophic worldviews, and religious systems), Epaphras sought the advice of Paul who was at that time in prison in Rome (in the early 60s).

When Paul received information about the problem in Colossae, a church which he had never personally visited, he wrote a letter focused on the lordship of Jesus. The letter is brief and is characterized by short sentences.

At about the same time, perhaps shortly thereafter, he wrote a more thoughtful treatise on the same theme—the lordship of Jesus and the importance of this concept for a proper understanding of the unity of the church. This is Ephesians, and as noted, may have been a circular letter intended to be distributed to several churches. Ephesians is characterized by long sentences and development of theological themes.

Factors that are often cited in demonstrating a close relationship between Ephesians and Colossians include (1) related literary and theological structure, dealing with the same general topic, (2) similar salutations and similar closings, (3) similar words and phrases (as many as 75 of the verses in Ephesians have a parallel in Colossians), (4) Paul's authorship, and (5) both were delivered by Tychicus.

In summary, both Ephesians and Colossians are among Paul's four prison letters. There are several similarities between the books. Colossians was written to combat a specific Christological problem. Ephesians was written (possibly as a circular letter) to stabilize the church (or churches).

Purpose of the Letter

The theme of Ephesians is found in Eph. 1:9-10, which says that the eternal purpose of God was to bring together everything in unity under the lordship of Jesus. This theme is reflected in various ways throughout the book.

General Outline of the Letter

The book naturally divides into two parts (as do many of Paul's letters). These are variously described as teaching and application, pedagogy and practice, explanation and exhortation. More detailed outlines are provided at the beginning of each chapter. Remember that one purpose of this study guide is to help the student develop the ability to read and outline the biblical text, first steps toward seeking the message and meaning of the text then in order to understand the message and meaning of the text for today.

1-3, God's plan for unity in Christ (theology)
4-6, God's plan as it is to be practiced in the context of the church (application)

Ephesians 1

[Note: it is suggested that the student read the introductory materials on pages 3-8 of this guide before beginning any individual preparatory reading and analysis.]

CONTENT

The outline and paragraphing included in the Content section of each chapter are only suggestions or guides. The student is encouraged to identify the paragraphs and subsections within each paragraph to assist in his or her own study. The division of the biblical text into paragraphs is fairly standard in modern translations. Note the brief salutation and the absence of typical elements of the Greek letter form. Paul immediately introduces the theme of the letter: God's saving work in Christ with the purpose of uniting all things in Christ.

Outline of the Chapter
1:1-2, salutation and greetings
1:3-14, God's saving work in Christ to accomplish his eternal purpose (vv. 9-10)
1:15-23, Paul's prayer that the readers understand the supremacy of Christ

STUDY HELPS

1:1-2. The salutation or greeting in the book is typically Pauline. The description of Paul as an "apostle of Christ Jesus by the will of God" appeals to his authority as an apostle, reminds of his commission as an apostle to the Gentiles, indicates that he was personally sent by Christ Jesus just as were the other apostles, and reminds that his apostleship is the fulfillment of God's will in his life. In those letters where Paul does not describe himself as an apostle (Philippians, 1 Thessalonians, 2 Thessalonians, and Philemon), it seems that he desires a more personal touch, basing such letters more on personal relationship and less on apostolic authority.

Apostle is from the Greek verb *apostello* which means "to send." An apostle is, literally, one who is sent. The term is most familiar in Scripture with reference to the Twelve (plus Matthias, cf. Acts 1), but is also used in the New Testament to describe those who were official representatives but not part of the Twelve (see Gal. 1:19, 2 Cor. 8:23, this use of the word is similar to ambassadors in 2 Cor. 5:20).

Christ Jesus combines the name Jesus (which means Savior; the name is Jesus in Greek, Joshua in Hebrew) and Christ, which is the Greek word used as the equivalent of the Hebrew Messiah. The Greek word means anointed or chosen. In Zech. 4:11-14, both the high priest and the king are described as anointed, indicating that the designation "Christ Jesus" combines royal and priestly functions. This is the primary point of the book of Hebrews. In the Old Testament, prophets were also anointed. "Christ Jesus" combines prophetic, priestly, and royal functions (cf. Hebrews 1:1-4), but whether the use of the designation intentionally calls attention to this, or whether it came to be a usual description among the first century Christians is difficult to discern.

Saints (holy ones) is a common way to refer to first century Christians. The description of the recipients as faithful is limited in New Testament letters. There is a manuscript variant with regard to the phrase "in Ephesus." The words are omitted in some ancient Greek texts, p^{46}, $\aleph^*$, B^*, and the text used by Origen and Tertullian. They are included in uncial manuscripts $\aleph i^2$, A, B^2, D, F, and G. As a result, Ephesians is often regarded as a circular letter, designed to be read in multiple churches, where the reader could insert the name of the local congregation during the public reading.

Grace and peace reflect a normal salutation. The normal greeting was "*charein*" meaning to be of good cheer. Paul used a similar word "*charis*" (grace). The use of peace would parallel the Hebrew use of "*shalom*."

1:3-14. This is one long sentence in the original Greek. I have reflected this in the outline above and in choosing to treat the notes over this section as a unit. Internal markers subdivide the section (the repetition of "to the praise of his glory" in vv. 6,

12, 14). Long sentences are characteristic of the book of Ephesians (1:3-14; 15-23; 2:1-10; 3:1-12, 14-19; 4:11-16; 6:13-20).

1:3. Blessed is from the Greek word that gives us eulogy (*eulogeo*). It is different from blessed (*makarios*) in the Beatitudes. The common letter form would open with a prayer, but here the blessing introduces a word of praise to God which describes the saving work that God has accomplished in Christ Jesus in order to fulfill God's eternal purpose. The prayer for the recipients is delayed until 1:15-23.

The God whom Paul praises (blesses) has blessed believers "with every spiritual blessing in the heavenlies in Christ." The concept of "the heavenlies" is not easy to understand. It is unique to this letter (1:3,20; 2:6; 3;10; 6:12). It is locative, neuter, plural, and is a substantive, an adjective functioning as a noun. The word apparently refers to a spiritual realm. Believers presently live in the realm "of the heavenlies" so it should not be understood as heaven. Other forces also live in this realm (1:20, 6:12, see comments on those texts).

1:3-6. God is the subject of the verbs in this section. What God has done has made a difference in the lives of the believers. He has blessed us, chosen us, predestined us, and favored us (made us acceptable). This is in accord with his will. Each of these verbs deserves attention.

Blessed and blessings are both from *eulogeo,* literally meaning to speak well. The blessings are "in Christ." This is a key concept through this section (v. 3, 4, 6, 7, 9, 10, 12, 13).

Choose is from *eklegoma*i. God is the subject of this verb. God's choice was made before the beginning of time (before the beginning of the world); God's choice focused on the location and the result, not on the who—chosen in him (in Christ) to be holy and blameless. A good way to describe this is to say that God's choice was covenantal, meaning that it extended as far as the covenant extends and no further. God calls all humanity in Christ. It is not possible for human beings to respond to God's call and remain outside of Christ. God's saving actions are in and through Jesus. (Remember that the theme of this section is God's saving work in Christ.) However, the covenant is not unilateral. It is an agreement between two parties. God initiates (he chooses from before time), but his choice is specific "in Christ" and thus extends only to those who are "in Christ;" and his choice is for those who are holy and blameless which is only possible through Christ, thus for those who depend on Christ for salvation. God makes this choice to accomplish his will. His will is to bring everything together under the headship of Christ (1:9-10), something that will also accomplish the restoration of humanity to relationship with God. That is possible only by dealing with sin. Thus, God's will is that we be again in his image (Gen. 1:26-27; 2 Cor. 3:18; Rom. 8:28-30; and see also Gal. 4:19; Eph. 4:13; Titus 2:14; 1 Pet. 1:15.) Understanding these points will help clarify the next verb Paul uses.

"In love" can be understood as part of the preceding phrase or part of the phrase that follows it. The Greek text does not have the punctuation that would help us decide—it is a context question. Predestined is from *proorizo*. This verb can be translated as predestined, destined, chosen, marked out, predetermined, ordained, or limited in advance. The verb is a combination of *"pro"* which means before or in advance, and *"horizo"* which is the word from which we get the word horizon. When one considers that the horizon is a line of separation (between the earth and the sky), one gets a sense of the meaning of this word. To set a horizon is to mark off a line of separation or distinction. This word must be understood as part of the context, not as a separate concept. It is one of several integrated truths in this section. Note that the object of the verb is corporate not individual. It does not say that God predetermined me, but that God predetermined his people (us, in the context of Ephesians 1). God chose a people who would agree to his covenant. As it were, God drew a line in the sand and gave human beings the opportunity to choose where to line up (free moral agency). Each person has to choose a side. God made his choice and predetermined in accord with two things— "in Christ" and "holy and blameless." Human beings have a choice to make. Will I choose to be "in Christ;" will I choose to be "holy and blameless?"

God predetermined (with the line of separation he drew in advance) that his will would be accomplished by making possible "adoption as sons." This is the "how" of God's purpose. It is "through (*dia*) Jesus unto himself." This is according to God's pleasure (that which pleases him) and his purpose (plan). This phrase reflects God's character and is paralleled in 1:7,9,11. God's actions are not based on knowing in advance what you and I will do, but are based on who God is, what pleases him, and his purpose in this world. (To remind the student of some related verses, see John 3:16-17; 1 Tim. 2:4; Tit. 2:11; 2 Pet. 3:9; 1 John 2:1-2.)

"To the praise of the glory of his grace" subdivides this section; the refrain is repeated at the end of each section of this long, extended Greek sentence (1:6,12,14). The refrain is followed by a connecting phrase that leads to the next section. This grace (*charis*) was graced (*charitoo*) to us in the Beloved, that is, in Jesus. *Charitoo* is translated in various ways in our versions: freely bestowed on us, made us accepted, as a free gift to us, especially honored us, highly favored us. The connection between the two Greek words is powerful, but is difficult to maintain in the translation. That God grants us status as sons and makes us accepted indicates again that the basis of our salvation (and the basis of God's actions to bless, choose, predetermine, and graciously favor us) is not in our actions, but in God's character or nature. All of this occurs "in Christ, in him, in the Beloved."

1:7-12. "In Him" we have blessings—redemption, forgiveness, grace, wisdom, insight, and knowledge. This describes our present state (present tense) based on God's past actions. Redemption is "to buy back" or "to be delivered" (see Rom. 3:24; Col. 1:14; plus Eph. 1:7,14; 4:30). Redemption is through Jesus' blood. Forgiveness is "sending away." Here the Greek word for sin (*paraptoma*) means a "side slip," either a lapse or a deviation from the standard. Paul does not use the more common word for sin (*harmartia*), perhaps indicating that the breadth of God's forgiveness corresponds to the richness of the grace extended in Jesus Christ. This grace was overflowed to us (*perissueo*), thus the translation, "lavished on us."

1:8-9. We receive knowledge, understanding, and wisdom as blessings from God. We understand the depth of the gospel. This knowledge is described as a mystery. In contemporary usage, a mystery is something unknown or inexplicable. In the New Testament, it is more often used to describe something previously unknown but now revealed. To see how this meaning is reflected in the context of Ephesians, compare 1:9;

3:3, 4, 9; 6:19. In Ephesians, the mystery is that everything and everyone—Jew and Gentile—can be united in Christ (1:9-10; 2:11-3:13), according to God's eternal purpose and will (1:6). This truth was not previously grasped, but has been revealed in Christ (3:3-4).

"In Him," ….
God blessed us
God chose us
God predestined us
God graced us
So that "in Him," we have….
Redemption, forgiveness, grace, wisdom, insight, and knowledge

---

1:10. God's eternal purpose has always been to unite everyone in Christ (*anakephalaiomai*, to bring together under a head). This is the central theme of the book—the teaching of Chapters 1-3, and the goal of the application in Chapters 4-6 (see esp. 4:1-6). While this has always been God's purpose, it was not accomplished until the time was right, in the fullness of the times.

1:11-14. In vv. 11-14, one can note another listing of blessings available only in Christ—inheritance, hope, word of truth, gospel, salvation, faith, Holy Spirit. Inheritance reminds that God has chosen us to be his people. Literally, the reading is "we were chosen as an inheritance." This again is by God's predetermination and is consistent with his eternal purpose. When God's purpose (all things united in Christ) is understood, the line of separation he made as a predetermination is also clear (those who are in Christ).

God (1) made the determination in advance, (2) freely allows us to choose or not to choose the covenant that makes it possible for us to be or not to be in Christ, and (3) did not make the choice or the predetermination based on his foreknowledge of the works or actions of any individual or individuals. Thus, the predetermination is not merit-based. Compare this idea to the disclaimers of Eph. 2:8-9: not of your own initiative, not of yourselves; it is a gift of God; it is not based on works and thus avoids human boasting.

1:12-13. It is possible that v. 12 refers to the Jews and v. 13 to the Gentiles (see 2:3, 11-14). An alternative understanding would see a reference to the apostles and subsequent believers, but the delay in Paul's apostleship and coming to be a believer makes it less likely that it would include himself in those who were "the first to hope in Christ." The refrain, "to the praise of his glory," is repeated in v. 12.

Salvation comes from hearing and believing the word of God, the truth, the gospel. Salvation is impossible without the gospel (the gospel of your salvation), a message that must be personally received and acted upon (obeyed, Rom. 10:16-17; 2 Th. 1:8; 1 Pet. 4:16-17).

1:13-14. This belief and obedience leads to receiving the promised Holy Spirit (cf. Acts 2:38-39). Baptism is in the Holy Spirit (1 Cor. 12:13). The Holy Spirit in the life of the believer is a seal, a sign of security, authenticity, and ownership, and is given only within the covenant. A seal is also a pledge, downpayment, earnest money. In modern Greek, it is an engagement ring. The Holy Spirit was promised as a comforter and presence that would come when Jesus ascended (John 13:16, 26; 15:26). The presence of the Holy Spirit is the promise of future resurrection (Rom. 8:9-11). All of this is "in him."

The presence of the Holy Spirit in the life of a believer is the promise or pledge of God until the time when God's choice of us as his inheritance is confirmed by the redemption of God's own possession (see Exod. 19:5, cf. Tit. 2:14). The third use of the refrain "to the praise of this glory" closes the section.

1:15-23. As explained previously, in the book of Ephesians the prayer that is typically included in the Greek letter form immediately after the salutation, does not appear until after the theme section. This prayer and intercession is one long sentence in Greek.

1:15-18. The reader should keep in mind the possibility that this is a circular letter, in which case Paul would write with reference to several churches. Faith can refer to personal faith or trust, a faithful manner of life in Christ, or the body of teaching, the doctrine (when used with the definite article). All of these are possible in the context. The ASV catches the third meaning in the translation, "the faith in the Lord Jesus which is among you." Since the article is used here, this meaning is perhaps best.

"Your love" has textual variants and is not supported by some of the earliest Greek manuscripts. It may be the result of a desire to standardize Paul's phrases (see parallels in Eph. 1:4 and Philemon 5). The variants do not change the overall meaning of the text, but it may be helpful for the reader to know about the variants since some translations may not include a reference to "love." Saints is the typical way to describe Christians.

Paul often prayed for the churches. Paul's prayer here includes thanksgiving and petition. The petition specifically mentions four things.

1:17-18. His prayer is that the recipients might be given the spirit of wisdom and revelation in the knowledge of God, and that the eyes of their hearts be enlightened. In the text, the word spirit is anarthrous (does not have the definite article). It may refer to the Holy Spirit, but is more likely a reference to the human spirit. A reference to the Holy Spirit makes this passage Trinitarian. The third person pronouns in vv. 17-18 refer to God the Father.

Paul prays that the recipients of the letter may have knowledge. This knowledge has three elements: hope, inheritance, and power. He prays that the recipients might know these three things. Hearts enlightened is parallel to 2 Cor. 4:4-6, and refers to receiving understanding. In this context, the heart is parallel to the mind which can be enlightened and can receive information. Specifically, Paul's prayer is that they may know "the hope of his calling, the riches of his glorious inheritance, and the greatness of his power." "His calling" refers to God's call to human beings. "His glorious inheritance" can be God's inheritance, the idea that we are his inheritance (1:11,14), although the "riches of the inheritance" seems to refer to our inheritance. The power God has made available to Christians was also demonstrated in Jesus' resurrection.

1:19-23. The power is immeasurable, surpassing, or extraordinarily great. It is for believers. The conditional nature of the covenant makes it essential that human beings participate in the salvation God has powerfully initiated in Christ. Because God's predetermination excludes no one, the gospel is inclusive. This does not lead to universalism. Because the covenant is conditional, some may be excluded (may choose to exclude themselves by rejecting the covenant). Christians are those who believe that God will be faithful to his covenant promises and thus submit to the covenant conditions.

God's power is immense. Paul uses four words in this context (*dunameos, energeian, kratous, ischuos*). God's power is exercised in Christ and through Christ. This power of God raised Jesus from the dead, seated him at God's right hand, put all things under Christ's feet, and made him head over all things to the church. The same power is at work in believers. What God has done for Christ in raising him and seating him, Christ does for his followers, cf. 2:5-6, where the same actions are preceded by *sun-*, signifying joint participation.

The resurrection of Jesus is an evidence of God's power at work. Our resurrection spiritually and our future resurrection physically are by the same power. Those who are looking for miraculous evidence of God's power at work have to look no further than the changed lives of those who have been raised to walk in newness of life (Rom. 6:1-6). God seated Jesus at his right hand "in the heavenlies." This word appears five times in Ephesians (1:3, 20; 2;6; 3:10; 6:12). The fullest explanation is in these notes at 6:12. Jesus was exalted over every other power and authority in every place and in every time.

God put everything in subjection to Jesus (under his feet). He is head over everything to the church. He is head of the church (Col. 1:18), but he has been exalted to a more expansive headship (Eph. 1:22; Col. 2:8). This metaphor is rich. The head gives life to the body; it controls, directs and guides the body.

The church (*ekklesia*) is an assembly called together for a specific purpose. The Greek word is used in the Septuagint (LXX) to translate the Hebrew *qahal*. Both terms refer to the people of God. In this text, the church is described as the fullness or completion of the one who fills everything in every way. What does this mean? It may mean that everything the church has it receives from Christ, Christ is filling the church. It may mean that the church is the final result, the completion, of God's saving work in Christ. It may mean that all of the saving work God has accomplished in Christ is exercised in the church since it was pointing toward the goal of unifying all things in Christ. To some extent, all of these are true. In the context, the last meaning is especially appealing. God's eternal purpose to unify all things in Christ is made possible through the saving work he has done in Christ and through Christ. The saving work of God is never exerted outside of Christ; it is always in Christ, the completion or fullness of Christ, so that the church reflects and responds to her head.

Ephesians 1: In Jesus Christ we can see....

God's purpose

God's promise

God's power

God's presence

God's pleroma

CHAPTER SUMMARY
God's Saving Work in Christ

God has blessed us, chosen us, predestined us, and favored us. All of this is "in Christ." In Christ we have redemption, forgiveness, grace, wisdom, insight, and knowledge. All of this is evidence of God's eternal plan and purpose to bring everything together in Christ. The beauty of God's plan is made clear when one considers that in Christ is inheritance, hope, the word of truth, the gospel of salvation, faith, the Holy Spirit as the seal of promise.

The Supremacy of Christ

I pray that you will have wisdom and knowledge to understand, to know the hope of your calling, to know the riches of the glorious inheritance, to know the power of God that works in you just as it resurrected Jesus and seated him as the ultimate authority and head over all things, head of the church, where the fullness of Christ is fully in view.

Ephesians 2

[Note: it is suggested that the student read the introductory materials on pages 3-8 of this guide before beginning any individual preparatory reading and analysis.]

CONTENT
The paragraphing included in the Content section of each chapter provides suggestions and guides. The student is encouraged to identify the paragraphs, and the subsections within each paragraph, to assist in personal study. The division of the biblical text into paragraphs is fairly standard in modern translations.

Outline of the Chapter
2:1-10, in Christ God saves us, moving us from death to life
      2:1-3, humanity's fall into sin
      2:4-7, God acted on behalf of humanity
      2:8-10, the covenantal relationship made possible by
      God's initiative is reflected by human response
2:11-22, reconciled and one in Christ
      2:11-12, the need for Christ
      2:13-18, the work of Christ
      2:19-23, the result of Christ's work

Observations about the Content of the Chapter
      2:1-22. The context of the chapter begins in Chapter 1 with Paul's description of God's saving actions in Christ, the blessings that come to believers as a result, and God's eternal purpose which is made evident in the church. God initiated all of this by grace (2:1-10), to accomplish his redemptive plan in Christ (2:11-22, 3:1-13). The truths set forth in 2:11-3:13 are described as a mystery (see 1:9-10) that has now been revealed (3:3-4). The mystery is the desire of God to redeem all humanity in Christ. God has acted, human beings must respond. This

is true because God's action in Christ is covenantal, just as was his relationship with human beings in the Old Testament.

Note the parallel structure of the two major sections of the chapter. A similar progression was used in the first chapter: God's saving work in Christ is needed, what God has done in Christ, the results of God's work in Christ.

STUDY HELPS

2:1-10. This section is one long sentence in Greek with the main verb in 2:5. (The sentence may encompass only vv. 1-7.) Therefore, the section should be understood as one topic or argument. The movements of the argument are (1) that all humans are spiritually lost and thus hopeless and helpless, vv. 1-3, (2) that God has acted in grace, vv. 4-7, and (3) the result or response in the faith and life of believers, vv. 8-10. Each of these three sections is treated separately below.

First, **2:1-3.** Three factors that are involved in the entry of sin into the world and the fall of humanity are the nature of the world system (the course of this world), Satan himself, and the tendencies of human nature (passions, desires). These verses describe humankind as dead in trespasses and sins, therefore in rebellion to and separated from God.

Second, **2:4-7.** In the midst of this situation, with no explanation visible within the experience of humankind, God on the basis of his love and mercy, in Christ (with Christ) made us alive, raised us, and seated us (exalted us).

Third, **2:8-10.** That salvation was initiated by God and that the saving work in Christ was accomplished by God without human help does not contradict the necessity of human response. God's grace demands response and a changed life that conforms to his purpose, described in this context as something prepared in advance. The covenantal relationship that is made possible by God extending grace must be reflected in human actions, described in this context as good works.

2:1-3. Passages that describe the recipients of the letter (including both Jews and Gentiles) as previously dead, walking in disobedience, and following human passions present a difficulty because it is at times hard to see how they apply to the experience of first-century Jews. See Titus 3:3 for another example.

Paul writes that they were dead (spiritually) because of trespasses (*paraptoma*, see comments on 1:7-12) and sins (*harmartia*, missing the mark, the more common Greek word for sin).
Those described in these verses formerly lived (literally,
walked, a common metaphor that refers to living and manner of
life) according to the principles or ways (*aion*, age) of the world
(*kosmos*). World does not refer to the entire created system,
but to the worldly way of thinking, the "world system" (cf. Gal.
1:4; 1 Cor. 3:1-3). They also lived according to (followed) the
ruler of spiritual powers of the air. This refers to Satan who is
the ruler of this world (cf. Jn. 12:31; 14:30; 16:11; 2 Cor. 4:4).
In the context, air (*aer*, the 'lower' air) refers to the domain of
evil spirits. They lived according to the ruler of the spirit that
works in disobedient people. "Sons of" is a Hebrew idiom that
says "of the same nature," as in sons of light, sons of darkness,
and similar constructions.

2:3. We all once lived to fulfill fleshly passions and desires and were thus deserving of God's wrath as were the rest
(of humankind). The contrast between "you" and "we" in this
text is perhaps parallel to the usage in 1:12-13 (see notes there).
The "we" may refer specifically to Paul and his associates, or it
may refer to the Jews. Applying the "we" more broadly, to
Paul and all of the recipients (perhaps in various local churches), the text makes clear that none are exempt from the need for
God's saving mercy and grace that he exerted in Christ Jesus.

The problem was rooted in human nature, so that all
humankind was deserving of and subject to God's wrath.
Nothing in the human creation was deserving of God's gra-
cious, loving, merciful action in Christ. The conclusion that
must be drawn from these verses is that all—you, we, the
rest—are lost and deserve wrath.

The tendency of the human nature toward sin is often
misunderstood, and deserves a brief explanation here. Humans
were created as dual nature beings, possessing both the divine
nature as those made in God's image and likeness, and a human
biological nature that allowed them to live in the world. Human beings were made to balance these two natures. In fact,
one way to describe what happened in the Incarnation is that
Jesus Christ came to this world as a human being, perfectly
balancing the tension between the divine nature and the human

nature. The problem of sin arose when the human nature was allowed to dominate and the divine nature was suppressed. The problem Adam and Eve faced and failed to conquer is still the human problem. In Christ, God made it possible to push the reset button and he dealt with the carnal human nature.

2:4-7. The contrast between vv. 1-3 and this section should grab our attention. The terrible condition of humanity is more than adequately handled with the rich mercy and the great love of God. God's mercy and love are the explanation for why he initiated a saving work through Jesus when human beings were dead in sin and totally undeserving. The explanation of what God has done, as described in Ephesians 1, is based in the character of God.

2:5-6. The human state, "dead in sin," is repeated from 2:1. God has acted in love despite the human condition. Three things are mentioned. All of them are preceded by the Greek preposition *"sun"* indicating "with," in this case referring to participating jointly with Christ in these actions. With Christ, God made us alive, raised us, and seated us. All of this is by grace, all of this is a part of God's saving work in Christ, a truth that is set forth in more detail in v. 8. That God made us alive refers to spiritual life restored in Christ. That God raised us with him refers to baptism (Rom. 6:3-11; Col. 2:12-13). In baptism, believers participate in the major events of Jesus' life: crucifixion, death, burial, resurrection, and exaltation. Believers share Jesus' life, suffering, and glory. That God seated us with him suggests the idea of reigning with him (Matt. 19:28; Col. 3:1; 2 Tim. 2:12). This action is described as occurring "in the heavenlies" (see notes at 6:12).

2:7. God did all of this to show (put on public display) his purpose in Christ, and his great love and mercy. There is an alternative to the "age" of this world. It is the age of God's righteousness extended to human creation in Christ Jesus.

2:8-10. It may be that this section of Scripture is one of the most misunderstood and most misused in the New Testament. Paul has made clear in the two sections preceding that the salvation sorely needed by humanity (2:1-3) has been made possible by God's love, mercy, and grace (2:4-7). Salvation was initiated by God. Salvation hinges on God's nature and God's actions. Salvation begins in and flows from God's nature; it is possible because of God's actions in Christ. Salvation has not been extended to humanity based on any human merit.

The basis truths set forth in this section were introduced in 1:11-14. First, God's predetermination (predestination) was made in advance. It was made simply by defining the line of separation, and was therefore made impersonally. Second, the impersonal nature of God's predetermination allows each individual to choose (or not choose) the covenant, to decide whether to share in Christ or not. Third, God's predetermination was not meritorious, that it, it was not made with a focus on the works or actions of an individual, based on God's ability to foreknow. In the text of Ephesians 2:8-9, these three points are summarized in three disclaimers: salvation is not of your own initiative, "not of yourselves;" it is a gift of God; it is not based on works and thus avoids human boasting.

"You have been saved" (repeated and expanded from 2:5) is a perfect passive participle. Salvation was not accomplished by believers (active voice), but is something done to them or for them (passive voice). God is the subject. The salvation in view is the same salvation that Paul has been describing for two chapters. The salvation involves grace (in the dative-locative-instrumental case; this is not an indirect object, so it is either locative "in grace" or instrumental "with grace"). The common translation "by grace" can be understood as instrumental, but it is important to note that grace is the means and that the action is done by another—God. To understand clearly what is said here, one must avoid personifying grace to make it the actor.

This salvation also involves faith (the preposition *dia* followed by the genitive case means because of, by, by reason of, through). In this text, grace and faith are not set as competing forces. God saves with grace and because of faith. In the context of this passage, it is not correct to ask what humans do. Salvation is applied to human beings by God because of faith. Grace and faith are together the instruments; both must be present for salvation to become reality. Salvation is freely extended with grace, but that by itself does not make salvation a reality in the life of a believer. Salvation is applied because of faith, but that idea has no meaning if salvation has not been extended. Salvation is a process, described as a covenant transaction; it is never unilateral. God deals with sin and fallen humanity through a covenant. In a process that is hard for us to understand, God offers the gift only to those who receive it.

God takes the initiative with regard to salvation and sets the boundaries, markers, and separations. Humans respond to the covenant offer because they believe God exists and that he faithfully keeps his promises (Heb. 11:6). Among the faith responses to God are worship, changed thinking, changed lives, obedience, service, and faithfulness.

2:8-9. Salvation is not of human doing. Grace and faith are not of human origin. The reference is to the whole process of salvation. Salvation is not within the power of human beings to accomplish. It is God's doing; it is a gift; it is not merit-based, that is, it is not based on human works or actions. No human can boast about salvation, as though we were somehow responsible for our salvation.

2:10. Because God is the one at work, the result is his work. We are his workmanship (Greek *poiema*). Some translate this idea to say that we are God's masterpiece. Four aspects of God's work are in view: our creation in Christ Jesus, created to do good works, God's previous preparations for us, God's power for our life of good works.

Excursus on Ephesians 2:8-10

Explaining the process by which the saving work of God in Christ Jesus comes to human beings is not easy. It has been attempted by many through the years. Faith and grace are both instruments. Therefore, God's saving work (salvation) can never by "only by grace," and equally it can never be "only by faith." The saving work accomplished in Christ has no value without the presence of faith. Since the "hard lifting" is done by God in Jesus (the grace part), perhaps the human response (the faith part) should be seen as a catalyst, without which the action cannot occur. Green can be made from two components—yellow and blue. Until you get both "instruments" in the same place at the same time, you have nothing even remotely related to the final outcome. You cannot look at yellow and declare that you have half of green. Nor can you look at blue at declare that you have half of green. Until you have both yellow and blue at the same place at the same time, you have nothing of green. You have only yellow and blue. I know the parallels are inadequate, but in the same way you cannot look at God's grace and declare that you have salvation (or even half of salvation). And you cannot look at human faith and declare that you have salvation (or even half of salvation.) Salvation is dependent on two things existing together. It is not correct biblically to say that God's grace carries salvation to a halfway point between God and man, and that faith carries salvation the rest of the way. Any such understanding is at heart a "works" system that makes faith a part of the power necessary for salvation. It does not matter whether your definition of faith requires only belief, only confession, only repentance, belief and baptism, or some other combination of faith, confession, repentance, baptism, and faithfulness, such an understanding is a works system if it sees human response as something that completes the action.

Thus, the two instruments, grace and faith, are both essential and both must be present for the salvation transaction to occur. Without the presence of both, you have nothing. An interesting illustration can be taken from the operation of a drawbridge. A functional drawbridge requires that both sides of the bridge operate simultaneously; this is the normal operation of a drawbridge. One side does not operate without the other. In a parallel sense, God's grace cannot operate without human faith; human faith is possible because of God's grace. The two work together, they cannot work separately. Of course, a part of the problem with the illustration is that God's grace was extended before any human response. The application is limited to the individual, and in any individual case, both grace and faith must be present simultaneously.

The text refers to salvation as a gift. Faith receives God's grace in Christ (cf. Rom. 3:22, 25; 4:5; 9:30; Gal. 2:16; 3:24; 1 Pet. 1:5). Mankind must respond to God's offer of grace and forgiveness in Christ (cf. John 1:12; 3:16-17, 36; 6:40; 11:25-26; Rom. 10:9-13).

Development of the Theme of Ephesians

God's saving work in Jesus...
- helps accomplish his eternal purpose
- takes away the barrier that blocks his eternal purpose
- unifies all things in Christ

2:11-22. The transitional "therefore" ties this section to what precedes it, introducing a new literary unit. This is the third major point of the section. The first was a summary of God's saving work in Christ Jesus to accomplish his eternal purpose (1:3-23), the second was God's saving work in Christ Jesus to deal with the human dilemma posed by sin (2:1-10). The focus now turns to God's saving work in Christ Jesus as God's means to unify all human beings.

2:11. The text is straightforward and easily understood. Remember (present, active, imperative) suggests something already known to the recipients. The Gentile Christians are to remember their previous alienation from God. Gentiles (*ethnos*, literally nations) refers to all non-Jews. Being non-Jews, they are called "the uncircumcision" by the Jews who are described as "the circumcision," referring to fleshly circumcision.

2:12. The text mentions five aspects of the alienation from God: separated from Christ, alienated from Israel, strangers to the covenants of promise, without hope, and without God. These descriptions may be designed to remind us of 2:1-3. Separated from Christ incorporates ideas such as "without Christ" or "not having Christ." Alienated suggests the idea of being excluded. The Gentiles were foreigners in regard to citizenship in Israel, and thus were strangers to the Old Testament covenants of promise. The word covenants in this verse is plural. In fact, there were several different covenants described in the Old Testament, each with different requirements, often given to different persons. The human condition without God is hopeless.

2:13-18. "But now" reflects a transition to a changed position. But is an adversative particle. "Now" is in contrast to the former state. This is contrast, moving from hopelessness to hope. Two groups are described—those far off (Gentiles) and those near (Jews). The Gentiles have now been brought near, in contrast to the position described in vv. 11-12 (see also v. 17). They have been brought near by the blood of Christ, a way of summarizing God's saving work in Christ as described before.

2:14. Three things are said about Jesus. First, he is the source of peace. Second, he has made both, Jew and Gentile, one. Third, he destroyed the barrier (the middle wall that divides or separates), making possible the unity of all in Christ, that is to say, in the church. The peace, unity, participation, and sharing of the Jew and the Gentile in the church is the focus of the extended section (2:11-3:13). Paul calls this the mystery now revealed (3:3-4).

In the context, two relationships are being restored to peace. First, the text speaks of peace between God and his human creation, the vertical relationship. Second, the text speaks of peace between human beings, the horizontal relationships of life. Jesus himself makes such peace possible. The peace between human beings is seen in the fact that both groups are now one. Being Jews or being Gentiles is now replaced by being Christians. To accomplish this, Jesus broke down the dividing wall, the wall of partition or separation (Greek *fragmos*; fence, barrier, or hedge). The reference is to the divisiveness that came through the separation defined and maintained in the Mosaic law. With separation removed, unity is possible.

2:15. To understand this often misunderstood verse, it is important to read the passage as literally as possible while seeking understanding. "(14) For he himself is our peace, the one making both one and destroying the middle wall of separation, (15) the enmity, by his flesh, by abolishing the law of commandments set forth in decrees...." The result of this action by Jesus was the creation in himself of one new man where there had been two before, thus making peace.

This verse has been problematic because in Matt. 5:17, Jesus said he did not come to abolish the law and the prophets. Which is the correct understanding? Did Jesus abolish the law, a frequent reading of Eph. 2:15, or did he not abolish the law according to Matt. 5:17? Unfortunately, despite a general insistence on harmonizing Scripture, a common approach is to begin with the conclusion already established. Eph. 2:15 is used as a proof text for abolishing the Old Testament law, and the conversation is ended without attempting to reconcile the two passages. What does Eph. 2:15 say in the context? Paul uses abolish in Rom. 3:31, 6:6, and Col. 2:14. It means "to make null and void" or "to cause to have no effect."

The passage has one main verb, with dependent participles following. Jesus is our peace, having made both one, having destroyed the middle wall of separation and hostility, having cleared away (abolished) the law of commandments as it was expressed in decrees or ordinances. The three aorist participles point to prior action, thus the translation uses present perfect participles. Note that Jesus destroyed the law of commandments as it was being expressed in various decrees and ordinances. This word (*dogma*, decree or ordinance) often referred to public decrees, decrees of a legislature or of rulers. When applied to the teachings of the apostles, it refers to right living. In the structure of the text, enmity is equated with the "law of commandments expressed in ordinances." The enmity was the result, not of the teachings of the Old Testament but of the interpretation (decrees or ordinances) of the Old Testament by the Jews. Nothing in Old Testament teaching required that the Jews establish a relationship of enmity with the Gentiles. In fact, the Jews were to be a light to the Gentiles to bring them to God.

Jesus' work in uniting, destroying separating walls, and abolishing hostility (and the law of commandments as it was being expressed in Jewish ordinances) did not demand changes in the Old Testament. In fact, the text of Matthew 5 that seems to contradict Eph. 2:15 goes on to note the problem with Jewish interpretations: "You have heard it said, but I say to you...."

The law fulfilled its purpose. Jesus came to fulfill the law. Faith does not nullify the law. In faith, the purpose of the law is fulfilled and upheld. The enmity and the dividing capacity of the law as it was being applied was abolished in Christ. The law finds its perfect fulfillment in the coming of Jesus Christ.

All of this Jesus did "in his flesh," that is, through his ministry which culminated in his death and resurrection. By these actions, he made "in himself" (emphatic construction) one new humanity. This was God's purpose—to unite all people in

Jesus (1:9-10). This God did in the church—a point that will be expanded in Chapter 3. He established peace (2:14).

2:16. He did this to reconcile both (that is, Jew and Gentile) to God in one body (the church) through the cross. By these actions, he killed the hostility. The focus is on eliminating the hostility. The hostility resulted from false separations based on false decrees. With the separation eliminated, reconciliation is possible, the reuniting of humanity through Christ. This reconciliation is "in one body." This may mean by the physical body of Christ, but it more likely refers to the body of Christ, the church. The cross was Christ's way to redeem fallen humanity. In his own person, and in the cross, he killed the hostility. The emphasis is on the results of Christ's work.

2:17-18. Jesus brings peace. He comes in peace; he preaches peace. He preaches peace to both Jew and Gentile so they can come to know genuine peace, without hostility, and with full access to the Father through the one Spirit. The preaching of peace is likely an allusion to Isaiah's prophecy (see 57:19 and 52:7). In Christ, in the body of Christ, all have continual access to God's presence.

2:19-22. The final part of the chapter explains the importance of what has just been set forth in vv. 11-18. This is not the end of the literary unit. Observe that the chapter division does not perfectly follow Paul's argument in this case.

2:19. The Gentiles who were formerly far off (2:11-12) are now included. Four metaphors speak to this shared participation: not strangers, citizens, household or family, temple.

2:20. The house or household of God is built upon the foundation of the Apostles and Prophets, meaning upon the teaching and proclamation of the good news by them as inspired spokesmen. In Old Testament prophecy, the coming Messiah was to be the cornerstone (Isa. 28:16; Ps. 118:22, see 1 Pet. 2:4-10).

2:21-22. The idea that God has a distinct people is communicated in various figures: nation (citizens), people (saints), family, building, body, temple. The focus is on the corporate nature of the church, the body of Christ in which and through which all people are brought together under the headship of Jesus. The verbs indicate sharing "with" others.

CHAPTER SUMMARY

There is no room for doubt about mankind's need for God's saving grace. Just look at the way we (and all people) have lived in the past. God in rich mercy and love acted when we were dead in sin, giving us life in Christ. When we consider both God's saving grace in Christ and our faith, we could never reach the conclusion that salvation is our doing. It is always a gift from God, it is never received on the basis of our actions, although in the eternal plan of God, we are God's "action pieces."

Thus, even when Gentiles were without hope, without Christ, without God, without connection to the promise, and without connection to the people of God, God in Christ made peace, brought unity, and gave everyone access to God's throne room. We are no longer excluded, we are citizens, we are family members, we are God's building, God's holy temple, God's dwelling.

Ephesians 3

[Note: it is suggested that the student read the introductory materials on pages 3-8 of this guide before beginning any individual preparatory reading and analysis.]

CONTENT

The paragraphing included in the Content section of each chapter provides suggestions or guides. The reader is encouraged to identify the paragraphs, and subsections within each paragraph, to assist in his or her own study. The division of the biblical text into paragraphs is fairly standard in modern translations. Some would make 3:1-13 one paragraph, but it seems easier to grasp the message by dividing the section as in the outline below. This section (3:1-13) is a continuation of the literary unit that began at 2:11 (2:11-3:13).

Outline of the Chapter
3:1-7, the mystery revealed, Jews and Gentiles together
3:8-13, the mystery reflects God's eternal purpose
3:14-19, Paul's prayer
3:20-21, Doxology

Observations about the Chapter
    3:1-21. The first part of the chapter (3:1-13) is a continuation of the literary unit that began in Chapter 2 (1:1-23; 2:1-10; 2:11-3:13). A summary of these units is (1) God's saving work in Christ accords with his eternal purpose, (2) the great need of all mankind, (3) the eternal plan of God unites all in one body.
    Some students divide the first part of the letter into six shorter units (1:1-14; 1:15-23; 2:1-10; 2:11-22; 3:1-13; 3:14-21). Note the progression of thought: (1) God's saving work in Christ according to his eternal purpose, (2) Paul's prayer to recognize the supremacy of Christ in the world and in the church, (3) the need for God's saving work, (4) the description of God's saving work and its results, (5) God's saving work is

the mystery revealed, (6) Paul's prayer that God's saving work will have its full impact. In addition to these two options (with three units and six units), other outlining options combine or further divide the paragraphs.

STUDY HELPS

3:1-13. It appears that Paul starts a prayer of praise at the beginning of Chapter 3, but then inserts a comment about the mystery before resuming and concluding the prayer in 3:14-21. Eph. 3:2-13 follow theologically on the themes of 2:11-22. Paul repeats the introductory phrase of 3:1 in 3:14 when he returns to the prayer. Ephesians is a "Prison Epistle." Paul was in prison when he wrote the letter. Paul had been specifically sent to the Gentiles (Acts 9:15; 26:16,18; Rom. 15:16; Gal. 1:16; 2:9).

This division of the text makes 3:2-13 a parenthesis that explains Paul's understanding and proclamation of the mystery, especially focused on his ministry to the Gentiles (cf. Col. 1:24ff for a parallel text focused on his ministry to the Gentiles).

3:2-4. Two long sentences characterize this section; vv. 2-7 and vv. 8-12 are both long sentences in Greek. The first class condition shows the author considers the statement true. The recipients knew about Paul's ministry and calling. "You have heard of the administration of the grace of God given to me for you." Administration (*oikonomia*) communicates that idea that Paul had been entrusted with the message of grace as a steward responsible for carrying the message to the Gentiles. He received this assignment by revelation, a possible reference to his experience on the Damascus road, the words of Ananias, his vision in Jerusalem (Acts 22:17), or his time in Arabia (Gal. 1:12, 17-18). Thinking of "administration" as "commission" may catch the meaning of the sentence.

Mystery, in this context, is not something unknown, but is rather something previously unknown but now revealed. The mystery is the existence of Jews and Gentiles together in Christ, in the church. The reference to Paul's previous writing on the subject could refer to a previous letter (now lost), but most likely in the context refers to 2:11-22.

3:5. The mystery was unknown (not revealed) in previous times, but has now been revealed. The mystery was revealed not only to Paul, but also to his holy apostles and prophets (see 2:20, also 4:11). "Holy" retains its basic meaning of those set

In Christ Jews and Gentiles are...
- co-heirs
- co-sharers
- co-participants in the promise

apart for a specific purpose. The revelation was by the Spirit. Since those of times past did not understand the mystery, the reference seems to be to New Testament prophets. The reference reflects the meaning of prophets as spokespersons or proclaimers more than as predictors of the future. The message was revealed to and proclaimed by these holy apostles and prophets.

3:6. The message (mystery) is that the Gentiles are now heirs together, members together, sharers together in the promise. Each description uses the "*sun*" prefix to make a compound word, describing the shared life in Christ, with Jews and Gentiles together. The construction with the "*sun*" prefix is similar to 2:5-6.

3:7. While Paul's conversion to Christianity was by God's grace, this verse refers to his appointment as an apostle to the Gentiles. He does not call himself an apostle, but rather a minister (*diakonos*, the source of the word deacon). Paul recognizes that his ability to share the gospel is not by his own power, but by the working of God's power (cf. 3:20-21; also 1:19).

3:8-12. In verse 8 begins another long sentence in Greek (3:8-12). Paul describes himself as the "most least" of all saints (Christians). See parallel descriptions in 1 Cor. 15:9 and 1 Tim. 1:15. Nonetheless, Paul received grace which enabled him to preach to the Gentiles the unsearchable (unfathomable, boundless, infinite) riches of Christ. (Compare the use of the word riches in Eph. 1:7, 18; 2:4, 7; 3:8, 16). God's grace was also powerful to make known (explain, ESV translates this as "bring to light," the verb is the root of our word photo) the plan of the mystery (plan is administration, stewardship, cf. 3:2). The mystery hidden in times past is attributed to God the Creator.

3:10. The result of the revelation and preaching is that God's many-faceted wisdom is made known. God's wisdom is made known through (the preposition *dia* with the genitive) the church. (For the same construction, see notes at 2:8, "through faith.") What was formerly not known of God's wisdom and plan (1 Pet. 1:12) is now visible in the church. This verse is sometimes used to prove that the church is responsible for evangelizing, that God's wisdom is made known 'by the church.' While it is true that the church has been commissioned to share the Good News, this is not a sufficient prooftext to support that claim. The context here is that God's wisdom in his eternal purpose is visible in bringing everything and everyone together in Christ. Modern church growth theory says it is easier and best to build a church with generally homogenous groups. God's wisdom says that the church is evidence of forgiveness, humility, patience, endurance, love, and peace because it brings together diverse groups in unity.

Another reason the verse should not be applied to evangelism that is done by the church is that the revelation of God's wisdom in this context is to rulers and authorities in the heavenlies (see 6:12 and notes there).

3:11-12. All of this accords with God's eternal purpose (1:9-10) to be realized in Jesus. This concept serves to tie the first three chapters of Ephesians together. The overarching theme is God's purpose in Christ Jesus. Because of what God has done in Christ, Christians have boldness and confident access (cf. Eph. 2:19; Heb. 4:16) to God through faith in Jesus (literally, the faith of him). The question comes up frequently in Paul's writings (especially in Romans and Galatians) as to the meaning of this construction, "the faith of Jesus." As an objective genitive, Christ is the object of faith and the phrase refers to our faith. As a subjective genitive, Christ is the subject of faith, and it refers to Christ's faithfulness in fulfilling God's plan.

3:13. Probably referring to his imprisonment, Paul is suffering. He describes that suffering as "for you," referring to the recipients of the letter. He says that his suffering will also result in glory to them. Therefore, they should not lose heart.

3:14-19. With the repetition of the phrase, "for this reason," Paul resumes the prayer (cf. 3:1). He bows before the Father, although writers are generally quick to notice that the passage refers to Father, Spirit, and Christ. Father and family are from the same root word. In heaven and on earth is an idiomatic way of saying "all" and should not be understood literally.

3:16-19. Paul's prayer is easily outlined based on the grammar in Greek. There are three purpose clauses (subjunctive followed by "so that," *hina*) and four aorist infinitives. The construction is as follows (omitting most of the prepositional phrases): "¹⁶ So that (*hina*) God would give you to be strengthened, ¹⁷ to reside Christ in your hearts through faith, ¹⁸ so that (*hina*) you may have strength to comprehend, ¹⁹ and to know, so that (*hina*) you may be filled."

The order is Purpose—Infinitive—Infinitive—Purpose —Infinitive—Infinitive—Purpose. Purpose: that God would give you power to be strengthened in your inner being by the Spirit, to reside Christ (so that Christ may reside) in your hearts through faith. Purpose: That you may be given strength to comprehend (grasp, receive) and to know Christ's unknowable love. Purpose: that you will be filled with this fullness of God. The last two phrasings are remarkable for their repetition: to know the unknowable, to be filled with God's filling.

"According to the riches of his glory" is consistent with Paul's frequent use of this phrase in Ephesians (1:7, 18; 2:4, 7; 3:8, 16). "Inner man" refers to the spiritual component of the human being. The outer man is the fleshly body (cf. 2 Cor. 4:16-18). Christ's indwelling is paralleled in the New Testament by references to the indwelling of the Holy Spirit and the indwelling of God in the church (Eph. 2:22; see also 1 Cor. 3:16; 6:19-20). This indwelling is by faith. Even though the recipients are described as rooted and grounded in love, there was still a need for more strength to be able to comprehend and know the love of Christ that is beyond (surpasses) knowledge. This knowledge was not uniquely available to a few; this is knowledge shared with all the saints.

The final purpose clause says "in order to be filled with all the fullness of God." The meaning of the word fullness (*pleroma*) must be determined by the context (cf. Eph. 1:23 and Col. 2:9). Generally speaking, fullness means completeness or entirety.

3:20-21. Paul's prayer of praise concludes with a doxology. "To him who is able" refers to God the Father. God's capacity is exceedingly abundant, much more, infinitely more, beyond any human thought or desire. God's capacity is according to the power at work in (energizing) believers.

Paul's prayer is that God's glory be visible in the church and in Christ Jesus. God's glory dwells in Christ. God's glory dwells in the church, the people of God. The glory and the wisdom of God are to be made known through the church, unto the end of the ages, forever and ever.

CHAPTER SUMMARY

I have been telling you about God's grace, revealed to me, the mystery that God has made known, his plan to bring everything together in Christ, all people as heirs, members, and sharers of the promise through the gospel.

I have been privileged to preach this gospel to the Gentles, to clarify the plan, to show how wise God was in his plan, because now everyone has security and confident access to God.

I praise God for all of this—I pray that you will be strong in the inner spirit, that Christ will dwell in your hearts, that you will be rooted in God's love (to know what is in reality unknowable). God is able to do so much more than we can ever ask or think! And it is all possible because he is at work in us, energizing us, making known his glory through Christ and the church.

Ephesians 4

[Note: it is suggested that the student read the introductory materials on pages 3-8 of this guide before beginning any individual preparatory reading and analysis.]

CONTENT

The paragraphing included in the Content section of each chapter is merely a guide. The student is encouraged to identify the paragraphs, and subsections within each paragraph, to assist in his or her own study. Generally, the division of this chapter into paragraphs is fairly standard across modern translations. Sometimes, 4:17-32 is treated as one paragraph. It is possible to divide 4:1-16 into smaller thought units.

Outline of the Chapter

4:1-16, encouraging the unity that leads to a functioning church, how to "walk" in the church

4:17-24, renouncing the old life and pagan ways for the new life in Christ, how to "walk" in the world

4:25-32, instructions for the new life

Observations about the Chapter

4:1-32. This chapter begins the practical section of the book, built around five admonitions concerning how one lives (*peripateo*, to walk, is a common idiom meaning to live) as a Christian (4:1, 17; 5:2, 8, 15). Christianity is based on what one knows; Christianity is demonstrated by how one lives.

The theme of Ephesians is God's desire to unite everything (all humanity) in Christ (1:9-10). The beginning of the practical section (4:1-6) echoes the theme. Unity is intentional, is to be pursued, and is encouraged by certain personal qualities or characteristics.

4:7-10. This section requires careful study to understand the what and why of the passage. The teaching is based on an Old Testament citation. The section sets forth the principle that Christ gives gifts to the church and thus introduces the following section.

4:11-16. This passage describes how a healthy church with healthy members should function, using the gifts that Christ gives. Important points include the purpose of leadership and the results of leadership.

4:17-5:20 urges the rejection of the old pagan lifestyles and the practice of the new life in Christ.

STUDY HELPS

4:1-6. "Therefore" points to what has gone before, probably the entirety of Chapters 1-3. The basis of our Christian life is what we know and believe about God's saving work accomplished in Christ Jesus.

Paul identifies himself as a prisoner of the Lord, not unusual since this is one of the letters Paul wrote from Roman imprisonment. The initial admonition is to walk (live) worthy of the calling with which you have been called. Christianity involves answering God's call and then living a "worthy" life. The following verses will describe several aspects of this life. Jesus taught that following him involved both a gateway and a way (Matt. 7:13-14). This section reflects the same truth.

4:2. Several virtues are characteristic of the worthy life (and necessary for unity, v. 3). These include humility (*tapeinophrosune*, lowliness or selflessness, literally means lowliness of mind), gentleness (*praotes*, meekness, the word refers to strength that has been tamed), and patience (*makrothumia*, longsuffering). "Forbearing one another in love" is a participial construction, meaning either that the previous items together make up forbearance, or that forbearance is the summary or capstone of the necessary attitudes. An important point is that the Christian life is lived intentionally.

4:3. Diligence is required to maintain unity. Another participle maintains the parallel construction: giving all diligence (*spoudazo*). Everyone is responsible for maintaining unity. Based on God's desire to bring all things together in Christ, it should be immediately obvious that this is unity in diversity. Unity and peace go hand in hand, and are necessary for a healthy church.

4:4-6. <u>One body</u> (only one body) refers to the church. This is the overarching theme of the book and the ultimate goal of God's eternal purpose (1:9-10). <u>One Spirit</u> refers to the Holy Spirit. The Holy Spirit's role in giving us inspired Scripture makes it possible for us to know God's calling, hope, Jesus and faith in him, baptism, and God the Father. <u>One hope</u> to which you were called; hope that comes from your calling. This phrase may be illustrative. As there is only one calling from God and only one hope that comes from that calling, so also there is only one body and only one Spirit.

The list of "ones" continues—<u>one Lord</u>, referring to Jesus Christ, indicates Jesus' deity with the connection of "Lord" to the Hebrew YHWH. The <u>one faith</u> is in the one Lord. <u>One baptism</u> refers to water baptism, which in the New Testament was always the result of faith in Jesus. Just as Paul connects the first three in the list, so also the second three are connected. Because there is one Lord, there is only one faith (in the one Lord), and there is only one baptism that results from the one faith in the one Lord. Paul's declaration that there is only one baptism excludes the first-century continuation of various baptisms for different reasons. By A.D. 60 Paul was able to write that there was only one baptism. Finally, unity is essential and must be maintained; unity is summarized in the phrase, "<u>One God and Father of all</u>."

4:7-10. The major point of these verses is that each Christian has received grace. The point is made in v. 7; vv. 8-10 are proof or support. Christ is the one who gives each person grace (notice the passive voice, "to each…was given"). Christ's role is reflected also in the citation from Psalms and in v. 11, "He himself." The church as a body functions because each member functions. Each member has a part to play (v. 16).

To each one is given grace, according to the measure of the gift of Christ. This construction could refer to Christ received as a gift (objective genitive) but more likely refers to Christ the giver of the gifts (subjective genitive). The evidence of grace in the life of the believer is the presence of the gifts received from Christ. This concept of Christ giving gifts is important since the gifts that are present in the lives of believers are often attributed exclusively to the Spirit, "gifts of the Spirit." Here is a corrective. Some gifts are given by Christ, perhaps through the Spirit.

4:8. The Old Testament citation is from Ps. 68:18. The picture is of a king returning victoriously and giving gifts. The second line of the quote differs from the Masoretic text of the psalm, apparently inspired by a commentary that is found in Jewish literature that says, "He gave gifts to me." The commentary applies the passage to Moses when he went up to Mount Sinai and came down with the tablets of the law. Paul's use of the psalm appears to refer to Christ's victory by which he conquered his enemies. After such conquest, the King gives gifts (see Col. 2:15; 2 Cor. 2:14-17).

4:9. While some have seen in this verse a reference to Jesus' descent to Hades after his death on the cross (see Acts 2:31 where *Sheol* likely means grave rather than Hades; see also a possible allusion to the same event in 1 Pet. 3:18-20), the reference is to Jesus' coming into the world (John 1:14; Phil. 2:7-8). How is it possible to go up (using the words in the citation and in Ps. 68:18) unless one first comes down? A literal reading of the verse makes the point clear: The one who has gone up is the same one who "first came down to the lowest parts of the earth" (*ges*, a reference to soil, land, ground). Hades is not a part of the earth. The reference is to Christ coming to earth in the Incarnation.

4:10. The one who came down is the same one who ascended far above the heavens to fill all things. To fill (*pleroo*) is to complete, satisfy, accomplish, end, or perfect. The word also appears in 1:23 and 3:19.

4:11-16. This paragraph may be one of the most overlooked passages of the New Testament. The contemporary church enamored with professionalism, attracting consumers, and hierarchical ministry structures needs to rethink the very nature of the church, beginning with these verses. Leaders exist to facilitate the ministry of the body. Every member has a ministry task and is thus a minister, erasing typical minister-laity distinctions. Members must be trained (equipped, prepared, mentored) for service and must be the primary work force in the work of the church. When each member uses his or her own gifts to accomplish the work, the tendency to "Accentuate certain gifts,

Boast about gifts, Compare gifts, and Define exact characteristics of gifts" is diminished.

4:11. He, referring to Christ, gave gifts to all. The correct use of gifts begins with those who have been gifted as leaders. The gifts that exist in the local church will never be used well until the leaders do their job. Based on the definite articles, four groups of leaders are mentioned: apostles, prophets, evangelists, pastor-teachers. The construction is the Greek "*men...de*" so that the first group serves as illustration of the rest. Few English versions reflect this detail, but many Spanish translations show the basic meaning: "he gave some apostles, others prophets, others evangelists, others pastor-teachers" (e.g., Spanish translations such as Reina-Valera, LBLA, NBLH, BHTI, and PDT). The meaning is this: as he (previously) gave some to be apostles, he has now given to others as prophets, evangelists, and pastor-teachers. These have in common the work in proclaiming God's message.

"Some apostles." While the word apostle (meaning, one who is sent) in the New Testament is not applied exclusively to the Twelve, in the context of Ephesians 4 it appears that the group in mind is the Twelve (cf. 2:20, 3:5), given as an example of how Christ give gifts to human beings for his purpose.

"Others prophets." Contextually (based on the *men...de* construction), prophets (again, cf. 2:20, 3:5) refers to a group of leaders that existed in the New Testament church. The word prophet (Heb., *nabi*) has three basic meanings: fore-tell (predict), forth-tell (proclaim or preach), and for-tell (herald, as a representative carrying the message of another). These may be seen as the past, present, and future of prophecy. The New Testament prophets were not always predictors of future events, although New Testament prophets that foretold future events are mentioned in Acts 11 and Acts 20. More often the New Testament prophets were spokespersons for God or simply proclaimers or preachers of the gospel message. In these non-miraculous meanings, it is not difficult to understand the existence of such leaders in the first century church. In the contemporary church, the problem with designating certain leaders as apostles or prophets is that there is almost always a sense of the miraculous, special revelation, and special authority, concepts which do not inhere in the words. The misuse of these two terms in the larger religious world of Christendom makes it unwise to use them in contemporary settings without explanation.

"Others evangelists." With the New Testament focus on the Great Commission and the need to share the gospel, it is surprising that the word "evangelist" appears infrequently in the New Testament (Eph. 4:11; Acts 21:8; 2 Tim. 4:5).

"Others pastors-teachers." This construction combines the functions of pastors (*poimenas*) and teachers. Biblically, there was only one group of leaders in each local church; they were at times called elders (*presbuteros*), at other times bishops (*episkopos*), and at other times pastors. The parallel use is reflected in Acts 20:17-31 and 1 Pet. 5:1-4, where these three ideas are attributed to a single group of leaders. The combination designation likely suggests the understanding that those who served as pastors were also teachers.

4:12. The purpose of these leaders was to equip the members for the work of ministry. The ministry of the local church is not the responsibility of hired staff. The ministry of the local church is the responsibility of the members. One church had a sign above the entry door, "Where every member is a minister." That slogan summarizes well God's plan for the local church. Leaders are responsible for training, mentoring, and being examples so the members can learn how to do ministry. The great power of the church (Eph. 3:20-21) is available through God's working in every member. The work translated "equip" is used in Mark 1:20 of mending nets. In the first century, the word was used to describe the work of doctors who mended broken bones. The basic idea is "to restore to usefulness." It means being ready to function. The task of leaders is to equip every member, so that the people of God will be ready for every good work (2 Tim. 3:17). A primary result of this work is the building up of the body of Christ (cf. 2:20). When Christians work together, the body is edified, is built up, and grows.

4:13. Others results include unity of the faith, knowledge of the Son of God, and mature Christians reaching a measure of Christ's maturity. The proper application of 4:12 will lead to the results of 4:13. Unity of the faith (when "faith" has the article) likely refers to the belief system or doctrine (teaching). Knowledge (*epignosis*) is not just mental, but is experiential. Mature (*telos*, sometimes translated perfect) means reaching the end or completeness, thus full-grown. Here it may mean fully-equipped.

4:14. Mature Christians are not whiplashed back and forth by every concept that comes along. For Christians who tend to follow after every new fad that comes along, the antidote is a solid foundation (edified) in faith, knowledge of Christ, and Christian maturity that seeks to become more and more like Jesus. Immaturity is described as child-like (cf. 1 Cor. 14:20).

4:15. The participial verb that begins this verse is interesting, literally it translates as "truthing." The meaning is not only speaking the truth but living the truth; it is applying the truth to every part of life, it is a life that corresponds completely to truth. The church, when it is "truthing," grows up in every way toward the head who is Christ.

4:16. The body, the church, working together in harmony, united, with every connection point functioning for mutual help, with the appropriate activity of every member—that church will grow and will go forward edifying itself in love.

4:17-24. The new literary section begins with another admonition related to the lifestyle of believers (to walk, a metaphor for "to live," that you no longer walk as the nations, Gentiles, pagans, heathen). The admonition is followed by several descriptions of the pagan lifestyle. "No longer" shows that some believers formerly practiced the lifestyle described (cf. 4:28). Paul describes the lifestyle to be avoided: worthless and futile thinking, darkened understanding, alienation from God, ignorance, hard hearts, callousness, sensuality, greed, and impurity.

Worthless (*mataiotes*) thinking is literally "useless, depraved, or vain." The way of thinking that characterized the unbelievers in the world was useless with regard to human capacity for understanding.

Darkened understanding (*dianoia*) is literally "being darkened the imagination, mind, or understanding." The phrase may be a repetition of the preceding thought—totally incapable of understanding.

Alienated or excluded from the life that is from God reminds of 2:12.

Ignorance is likely self-willed. Ignorant because they choose to be ignorant. This connects to hard (*porosis*, stupid, callous, blind) hearts.

4:19. Being past feeling (*apalgeo*, apathetic, dulled, thus callous), and giving themselves to sensuality (*aselgeia*, wantonness, lasciviousness, filthiness). Given to an occupation (*ergasia*, working, activity) with uncleanness (*akatharsia*, with every type of unclean activity), with an attitude of greed (*pleonexia*, avarice, covetousness).

4:20. Concluding the ugly description of the lifestyle of the pagans, Paul reminds that the Christian lifestyle is exactly the opposite. You did not learn Christ this way! Paul seeks to make clear the contrasts between the two lifestyles.

4:21-24. The first class condition is considered true from the author's viewpoint. The recipients of the letter had heard about Christ and had been taught the truth about him and in him. That truth included the need <u>to put off</u> the old self, that is the former way of life that was corrupted due to deceitful desires; <u>to be renewed</u> in mind; and <u>to put on</u> the new self that is created in God's likeness with righteousness and holiness.

The passage has three aorist infinitives—to place away from oneself (*apotithemi*), to be renewed (*ananeoo*), and to put on (*enduo*). These provide Paul's major points concerning how one seeks and finds the new life in Christ. Laying aside the previous life refers to repentance (changed thinking and changed lives). The previous way of life was corrupted by deceitful desires. It is not enough to eliminate faulty thinking, it must be replaced. The second infinitive refers to renovated thinking. Putting on the new self (literally man, a Greek word that can refer to both male and female) calls to mind Paul's description of baptism in other passages (cf. Rom. 6:1-6). The concept of "putting on" also appears in Gal. 3:26-27 with reference to baptism (cf. Rom. 13:14, Col. 3; James 1:21; 1 Pet. 2:1 for other uses of this same Greek word). The new self is re-created in God's likeness and is characterized by righteousness and holiness.

4:25-32. The initial "therefore" refers to what has gone before. Notice the repetition of "putting away" (the same verb as used previously). The aorist participle shows previous action, thus "having put away…" The participle, because it is connected to the imperative "speak," also has imperatival force. A commitment to the truth in Christ (v. 21) means putting away falsehood and speaking truth to one another. Speaking truth to one another is not only based in the decision to "put away" falsehood, it is also necessary to maintain the nature and function of the body where we are members of one another (cf. 3:6), where we belong to one another (cf. Rom. 12:5). Christians are not saved in isolation, Christians cannot stay saved in isolation.

4:26-27. The rest of the chapter continues a series of instructions using present imperatives. When a present imperative has a negative modifier, the construction often means to stop an act already in progress, but the continuous nature of the present tense can also refer to acts that are so common that they are in a sense continuous in the human experience. (In 4:25, the commands were to put away falsehood and to speak truth.)

4:26. This verse begins with two imperatives in a citation from Ps. 4:4. When anger is appropriate (be angry is an imperative), be careful that it does not lead you to sin and that you do not let it smolder within you for a prolonged period, since such only gives the devil a possible foothold. The second imperative is "do not sin." "Do not let the sun go down on your wrath" is a third person imperative. Since the Jewish day began at sundown, this instruction means that one should not allow the day to begin with anger in control and Satan lurking near. Again, the point is that one should not allow anger to remain long in one's life. This instruction relates to forbearance in 4:2.

4:27. This verse begins with "not even" (*mete*), following by the imperative "give." A smooth English translation reflecting the imperatival force could be, "Do not let the sun go down on your wrath, not giving the devil even the least opportunity (literally, place)." Devil is *diabolos* (literally, to throw across), perhaps referring to Satan casting accusations.

4:28. "The thief, no longer let him steal (third person imperative) but rather let him work hard (third person imperative, from *kopiao*, become fatigued)." The participle continues the imperatival force, "working (*ergazomai*) that which is good so that he has something to share with the needy." This verse reflects the changed life that is being described in this context.

Those who used to be thieves are to stop stealing and do honest work with hearts focused on helping others rather than hurting others.

4:29. "Do not let any worthless word come forth (*ekporeuomai,* third person imperative) from your mouth" contrasts with worthless (*sapros,* rotten, bad, corrupt) words. Rather, Christians speak words that are good for building up, speaking what is needed in order to give grace to those who hear. Here the word grace is not used to refer to saving grace, but to blessings or gifts.

4:30. Do not distress (imperative, from *lupeo,* to cause grief or sorrow) the Holy Spirit with which you were sealed (1:13) to the day of redemption (*apolutrosis*). The day of re-demption is likely the coming of Jesus.

4:31. The third person imperative (*airo,* to lift, to take away, to remove, to put away) has the sense of "let these be removed" from the life of the Christian: bitterness, wrath, an-ger, clamor, slander, and malice.

4:32. The imperative (*ginomai,* to be) is followed by two participles that partake of the imperatival force: be kind, well-compassioned, favoring one another. The favor Christians show to one another is the same favor God has shown to us (*chari-zomai,* the verb has the same root as *charis,* grace). The com-mon translation is that we forgive as God has forgiven us in Christ. Christians are imitators of God.

CHAPTER SUMMARY

If you understand God's plan for unifying all things in Christ, you will want to live in a way that reflects his calling in your life, with attitudes of peace, maintaining unity just as eve-rything about God reflects his desire for unity—God, Christ, the Holy Spirit, faith, baptism, hope, the church. Unity doesn't depend on you. God gives the gifts necessary to make it hap-pen. He has given certain leaders gifts to help the church work, to edify the church, to develop unity of faith, to know His Son, and to mature into his image.

Following God's plan keeps us from becoming unstable and deceived. God's plan lives out love, looks to Christ, and unites the body with each member working and encouraging and supporting and helping the others. Each member has a task, and the church grows and is built up in love.

If you understand God's plan, why would you want to keep living in darkness like so many in the world do? They are beyond help—vain thinking, without understanding, ignorant, hard-hearted, impure. That is not the way of Christ! In Christ, truth leads to a new life of justice and holiness. Be careful about your life! Watch your talk, your anger, your greed, your selfishness—we are all part of the same unified body of Christ!

If you forget how God sealed you and guaranteed the promise with his Spirit, the Spirit will be sad. Get rid of the bad stuff—remember how God has pardoned you and be equally generous to others.

Ephesians 5

[Note: it is suggested that the student read the introductory materials on pages 3-8 of this guide before beginning any individual preparatory reading and analysis.]

CONTENT

The paragraph divisions included in the Content section of each chapter are merely guides. The student is encouraged to identify the paragraphs, and subsections within each paragraph, to assist in his or her own study. Generally, the division of this chapter into paragraphs is fairly standard across modern translations.

Outline of the Chapter
[4:17-32, the new life in Christ, no longer "walking" as the pagans]
5:1-7, walk in love
5:8-14, walk in light
5:15-21, walk in wisdom, filled with the Holy Spirit
5:22-33, the Christian household, wives and husbands

Observations about the Chapter
     5:1-21 is a continuation of 4:17-32, giving instructions about how to walk in the Christian life. The outline above is built around the repeated use of the Greek word *peripateo*, to walk, meaning "to live." The word occurs five times in the context.
     5:22-33 is the first of three sections that describe family relationships in the context of the Christian life.

STUDY HELPS

5:1-14. The imperative (be, from *ginomai*) is repeated from 4:32, as though 5:1 serves as a summary of the preceding section, perhaps of 4:20-32, or of 4:25-32. Our word mimic is from the Greek word for imitators. Walk (imperative) is a

literal translation and is the usual word to describe lifestyle
and way of living.

The Christian must learn how to live...
In the church, 4:1-16
In the world, 4:17-32
In the family, 5:21-6:9

5:2. Christians walk in love because they have been
loved by God (not a bad summary of Ephesians up to this
point). Christ evidenced his love by giving himself as an offering (*prosphora*) and sacrifice (*thusia*).

5:3. The connection between the imperative, "walk
(live) in love," and what follows is not clear. Does Paul turn to
other matters in vv. 3-6, or is he describing what it means to
genuinely live in love? Love is more than emotion, love is
demonstrated in actions. What kinds of actions show love?

Do not let there be a hint of immorality (*porneia*), impurity (*akatharsia*), or covetousness (*pleonexia*, greed) among
you. Immorality is a broad category that includes various kinds
of sexual sins. "Let it not be named" is another imperative.
Such things are not fitting for Christians and are the opposite of
loving actions.

5:4. There is not a written verb in this verse. The verse
depends on and continues the prohibitions of the previous
verse. Grammatically, the things mentioned in v. 4 continue
the list from v. 3. This translation conveys the sense and the
connection: "Let the things that are not fitting not be named
among you, immorality, impurity, and covetousness; neither
filthiness (obscenity), foolish talking, and vulgar witticism
(crude, ribald jokes) which are not proper, but instead gratitude." How we act is an indication of our love; how we talk is
equally a measure of our love. Love is more than an emotion;
love is shown in attitudes and thoughts.

5:5. You can know with certainty that every immoral,
impure, and covetous person (reflecting the list in v. 3) does not
have an inheritance in the kingdom (cf. 1:11,14). Covetousness

is identified with idolatry (cf. Col. 3:5). In this verse is the only reference to the kingdom of God in Ephesians (cf. 2:2 where the word kingdom refers to the dominion of evil).

5:6. Let no one deceive you (third person imperative, from *apatao*, delude or cheat) with empty words. The things mentioned bring God's wrath upon the sons of disobedience. Disobedience to God in these matters or any others is the opposite of a life characterized by love.

5:7. I prefer to make a literary break here (as in the outline above), based on the repeated use of the verb "to walk," but the continuation of Paul's thought pattern makes the break a little less likely. The argument or thought builds throughout the section 5:1-14. Therefore (*oun*, literally then), do not be participants with them. The imperative (from *ginomai*) is repeated from 4:32 and 5:1.

5:8. This verse once again contrasts the former state or practice with the present (then, now). They were formerly darkness, now they are light. The imperative (walk, *peripateo*, meaning to live) in this verse instructs the readers to live as children of light. Children of light are not in darkness, they discern what pleases the Lord, they bear good fruit, they expose shameful things. "Children of light" contrasts with "sons of disobedience" (v. 6).

5:9-14. The fruit of light is goodness, righteousness, and truth. "Fruit of the spirit" is in manuscripts p[46], D[c], and I, while "fruit of light" is the obvious choice in the context, and is supported by p[49], ℵ, A, B, D, G, and P.

5:10. The participle (*dokimazo*, discerning, proving) continues the thought from preceding verses. It connects to the verb "walk" (live) and thus has the force of the imperative: discern what is pleasing to the Lord.

5:11-13. Do not participate (literally, fellowship with) the unfruitful works of darkness. Light bears fruit; darkness is unfruitful. It is not enough to refuse to participate, the imperative form demands that believers expose (*elegcho*, convict, convince, show the fault, rebuke, reprove) such works of darkness. Such things are shameful, even to talk of them is shameful, thus they need to be exposed by the light and thus become visible.

5:14. The quotation may be an early Christian hymn, or may be loosely based on some passages from Isaiah. The point is that Christ brings light.

5:15-21. The repetition of the verb "to walk" (to live) is in the indicative. However, coupled with the imperative to watch out, it has imperatival force. Christians must walk in wisdom, not as unwise persons.

5:16-17. Living wisely includes buying up and using well (*exagorazo*) your time (opportunity, occasion) because the days are evil. The opposite of foolishness is to understand the will of the Lord.

5:18-21. The two imperatives in 5:18 are opposites (foolish talk and thanksgiving, 5:4; light and dark, 5:8ff; fruit and fruitlessness, 5:9, 11; wise and unwise, 5:15; drunk and filled with the Spirit, 5:18). The imperatives of 5:18 lead to five explanatory participles.

"Do not get drunk, but be filled with the Spirit." The contrast may be designed to point to that which controls a person. The five participles that follow are "speaking, singing, making melody, giving thanks, and submitting to one another." These describe the life filled with the Spirit, or they describe ways to allow the Spirit to fill one's life. Many translations fail to honor the parallel grammatical construction, choosing instead to change the verbal form and use an imperative in v. 21. All of the participles have an imperatival force, building from the imperative, "be filled with the Spirit." My preference is for translation that shows the parallel verb forms of the original language.

5:21. The participle is reflexive, with the phrase "to one another" indicating that each one is to submit to the others. Submission is a reality of life. The word, in a military sense, means obedience within a chain of command. It can be applied in many other social contexts. Submission does not imply inferiority or inequality of worth. Submission simply honors the order that exists. Here it speaks to mutual submission as a characteristic of the spiritual life. The literary unit that follows (5:22-6:9) should be read in the context of mutual submission. Such mutual submission is done out of reverence to Christ.

5:22-33. In the literature of the first century, it was common to list mutual responsibilities between members of a family, including slaves. In the New Testament, these responsibilities are based in the fact that Jesus is Lord. In Ephesians, Paul treats three family groups that have reciprocal relationships and responsibilities, mentioning first the members of the groups that were considered weakest and in most need of protection. In the context of being filled with the Spirit, it may be Paul's purpose to show how the Christian life makes such relationships into spiritual relationships where each person is focused on responsibilities more than rights.

5:22-24. Three verses are devoted to instructions for the wives. Verse 22 has no verb, being a continuation of the thought in v. 21: literally, "the wives to their own husbands as to the Lord." The support for this short reading is minimal but early. Later witnesses add verb forms to the verse. With no verb present, the meaning of the verse depends on the participle of v. 21. Wives are to submit (*hupotasso*, the verb used in v. 21) to their own husbands as to the Lord, but this is not communicated with an imperative. (The only imperative in the extended passage of 5:22-33 is for the husbands in v. 25.) Submission "as to the Lord" does not suggest that a husband has the same authority as the Lord, but that the relationship and submission is based on relationship with Christ. "As to the Lord" in v. 22 is parallel to "in reverence" in v. 21. All Christians willingly submit to legitimate authority (cf. Rom. 13:1-3).

"Submit yourselves" is a concept that deserves expansion. Some translations use "be subject." The basic idea of *hupotasso* is to arrange things in order, thus to subordinate, to establish the order. In the active voice, the word means to put in subjection. In the passive/middle, it means to subject one's self, to obey, to submit to the control of another, to accept admonition or advice. These meanings provide helpful context for the admonition that resides in the participle in v. 21. This wide range of meanings should soften the harsh expectations and the hard attitude that some husbands exhibit based on v. 22. This verse does not make the wife a servant without rights. The verse exhorts a wife to recognize God's order and to be obedient to the (loving) control and advice of her husband who also wants what is best for his wife (cf. 5:25-28.)

5:23. The reason for the wife's submission is given in v. 23: the husband is the head of the wife as Christ is the head of the church. The use of the plural "husbands" in v. 22 (the correct and normal grammatical construction) makes it easy to forget that this is about the specific relationship between a husband and a wife, not about the relationship between men and women in the church. The relationship between Christ and the church is described in the Bible as like the husband-wife relationship. Christ is described as the head of the church, guiding, leading, instructing, saving. The church is the body of Christ, and later in the passage in a parallel thought, the husband is to love the wife as his own body. A husband, as head of his wife, is given a leadership role by God that is parallel to Christ's leadership role in the church. The leadership a husband should demonstrate in the home and family is servant leadership. It is functional leadership.

5:24. The church submits (is subject, obeys) to Christ, and in the same way a wife submits to the husband. Of course, the difference between Christ and the husband is that Christ is the perfect head and that the husband is imperfect!

5:25-30. The husband is to love his wife (in the context, the plural which is demanded grammatically is better understood as an individual responsibility in the context of a personal family relationship). This verb (love) is the only imperative in the passage.

Christ did several things on behalf of the church: he gave himself up for her, so that he might sanctify her and cleanse her, and so that he might present her without impurity, holy and without blemish. Jesus accomplished these things in his sacrifice, making possible the holiness and beauty of the church. Husbands are to love their wives in the same way. The husband loves his wife in the same way that Christ loved the church when he is willing to give himself for her (with a self-sacrificial spirit). The loving husband is committed to the holiness of his wife, recognizing that he is responsible for her splendor and beauty. The observation is likely right: more of the problems in marriages today come from husbands who fail to love their wives than from wives who fail to submit to their husbands.

5:28. A husband is to love his wife as his own body (as much as he loves his own body, as much as he loves himself).

"In the same way" reminds that Christ's love for the church was his love for his own body. A husband and wife become "one body" (Gen. 2:24). A husband who loves his wife is demonstrating how much he loves himself. The opposite is not said in the text, but should perhaps be stated here for clarity: A husband who fails to love his wife does not love himself very much.

5:29. Love for self is the normal state of things: people do not hate their own bodies (literally, flesh). On the contrary, we take care of our bodies. We nourish our bodies and cherish them, which is exactly what Christ does for his body, the church. A husband should nourish and cherish his wife.

5:30. Christ nourishes and cherishes the church because it is his body. We are members of that body. Therefore, Christ nourishes and cherishes us as members of his body. This thought summarizes well the message of Ephesians.

5:31-33. Gen. 2:24 is quoted from the Septuagint (LXX). The mystery (previously unknown but now revealed) is exceedingly great (*megas*, large, wide, big). The mystery (of a man and woman being one body, Gen. 2:24) is difficult to understand. Even more difficult is the fact that Paul refers to the oneness of Christ and the church, with the church identified as the body of Christ, so that Christ and the church are one body.

5:33. On the basis of this profound concept, every husband should love his wife as he loves himself, and every wife should respect (*phobeo*, literally fear, but in this context the word means to reverence) her husband. The husband is commanded to love his wife. Wives are instructed to yield to and respect their husbands.

CHAPTER SUMMARY

The instructions in this chapter call attention to the fact that you have to be careful how you live. Loving God as God has loved us means we avoid immorality, impurity, dishonesty, and useless words. These actions do not characterize the way of Christ. These are the things that lead to God's wrath. Don't do what you used to do. Now you live in light, you bear fruit, you know what pleases God, so it is time to be wise and diligent in how you use your time here on earth, seeking to do God's will.

You can avoid drunkenness and enjoy God's Spirit by speaking to one another in your songs, by singing and praising, by giving thanks, and by submitting to each other.

Submission also guides relationships in the home. Wives are submissive to husbands and respect them. Husbands demonstrate their submission by loving their wives, doing everything necessary for the wellbeing of their wives, serving, even being willing to sacrifice themselves. Husbands and wives are one body, and it is only natural to love your own body. (When Christ loves the church, he is loving himself; when the church respects Christ, it respects itself. These ideas are a great mystery indeed!) The wife must respect the husband, and the husband must love the wife.

Ephesians 6

[Note: it is suggested that the student read the introductory materials on pages 3-8 of this guide before beginning any individual preparatory reading and analysis.]

CONTENT

The paragraphs included in the Content section of each chapter are merely guides. The student is encouraged to identify the paragraphs, and subsections within each paragraph, to assist in his or her own study. Generally, the division of this chapter into paragraphs is fairly standard across modern translations.

Outline of the Chapter
6:1-4, children and parents
6:5-9, slaves and masters
6:10-20, Christian warfare against evil
6:21-24, final greetings

Observations about the Chapter
6:1-9 continues the treatment of family relationships (wife-husband, 5:22-33; children-parents, 6:1-4; slaves-masters, 6:5-9).

6:10-20 introduces what appears to be a new subject, but the passage has several connections to previous parts of the book. Especially obvious is the connection to Paul's earlier references to "the heavenlies" and to authorities and powers.

6:21-24 is a typical concluding section with personal comments and a final salutation. The absence of a large number of personal comments and personal greetings may reflect that Ephesians was a circular letter, intended for multiple congregations.

STUDY HELPS

6:1-4. The second family grouping (children-fathers) begins by addressing the weaker group. Children (no specific ages are specified by this word) are to obey (imperative, from *hupa-kouo*) their parents (*goneus*). "In the Lord" means according to the Lord's instructions or because the children are Christians (in the Lord). Parental authority is God-given, as are other spheres of authority, e.g. in the church and in human governments. The command is not based on whether the parents are Christians or not, although the context of this section suggests a primary application to the Christian home. Jesus taught about conflicts between children and parents based on conflicting allegiances (Matt. 10:34-39). The obedience of children to their parents is right (*dikaios*, just).

6:2-3. The quotation is from the Ten Commandments (cf. Ex. 20:12; Dt. 5:16), followed by the observation that the commandment to honor father and mother is the first commandment that had a promise attached to it. The promise is specifically cited in the continuation of the citation in v. 3.

6:4. The Greek text has "fathers" although some modern translations say parents. The construction of the passage is that in each of the three groupings, those with limited social rights and power are addressed first (wives, children, slaves), and then those with power in the society (husbands, fathers, masters). Fathers is the preferred translation. The instructions are especially applicable to fathers. Do not provoke to anger (imperative, from *parorgizo*) your children. The opposite of causing anger in our children is to nurture them (*ektrepho*, cherish, train) with education (*paideia*, training, tutoring, focused on teaching) and correction (*nouthesia*, admonitions, warnings). Fathers have a significant responsibility in the spiritual growth of their children.

6:5-9. The third family grouping follows the same pattern as the previous two, beginning with instructions to those with less social standing in the first century culture. Slaves (*doulos*) refers to household servants. Slaves are to obey (imperative, from *hupakouo*) their masters. This is the same word that was used in the instructions for the children (6:1). Wives were not instructed to obey. Wives were instructed to submit and to respect. The reference to human masters (masters according to the flesh, *sarx*) reminds that there is a heavenly master. Christian slaves are to obey human masters with fear (*phobos*, cf. 5:33 where the same word means respect) and trembling (*tromos*). "Fear and trembling" is an idiom; it can indicate fear but is also used to mean respect (1 Cor. 2;3; 2 Cor. 7:15; Phil. 2:12). In sincerity (*haplotes*, singleness, without hypocrisy, generosity) of heart, as to Christ (cf. 5:22).

6:6-7. These verses explain the phrase "in sincerity." Do not act in such a way that you are always calling attention to yourself and wanting to be watched or that you are seeking to please human beings, but rather as serving and pleasing Christ, doing God's will with vitality (*psyche*), giving your service willingly (*eunoia*, literally of good mind) as to the Lord and not to men.

6:8. Whatever good thing a person does, that person receives recompense from the Lord. This truth applies whether a person is a bondservant or is free. Christians seek to serve others without expecting reward or recognition, knowing that God is the one who sees and rewards good deeds (cf. 2:10).

6:9. Masters (*kurios*) are to use the same principles and guidance in how they treat their slaves. Do (imperative, from *poieo*) the same things, giving up (*aniemi*, letting up, forbearing) threats (*apeile*, menacing). The reason masters treat slaves well is that they recognize that there is an impartial heavenly Master who is Master of all—both the master and the slave.

6:10-20. "Finally" (*loipon*, what remains, as to the rest) indicates a transition either to the conclusion of the book or to Paul's final point. The context suggests the theme used in the outline above: Christian warfare against evil. The battle described is waged in this world but is not against flesh and blood. This battle is against rulers, authorities, cosmic power, and spiritual forces (cf. 1:21, 2:2-3, 3:10). Therefore, it is a spiritual battle (cf. 2 Cor. 10:3-5).

6:10. The first imperative of several is "be strong" (*endunamoo*) in the Lord in the power (*kratos*) of his might (*ischus*). The present imperative carries the sense of "be continually empowered." Christians make a choice concerning the powers that guide and control their lives. Three different Greek words that deal with power or strength are used in v. 10. (In 1:10, these three words plus a fourth, *energia*, were used.)

6:11. Put on (aorist imperative, *enduo*) the full armor (*panoplia*, panoply) of God. This is the second imperative in the sequence. "To be able (*dunamai*) to stand (*histemi*) against the trickery (*metodeia*, our word methods, meaning wiles, deceit) of the devil (*diabolos*, referring to Satan)." The armor is more defensive than it is offensive, perhaps because Jesus has already settled the ultimate outcome even though the battle continues in the lives of individual Christians.

6:12. This verse explains the importance of following the instructions in v. 11. The struggle (*pale*) is not against flesh and blood (literally, blood and flesh, meaning human beings, cf. Heb. 2:14). The present tense conveys the sense of continual struggle. The struggle is against rulers (*arche*); against authorities (*exousia*); against the rulers of the world (*kosmokrator*, the one having power in or power over the world, world ruler, controller) of the darkness of this age; against the spiritual powers (literally, this is an adjective functioning as a noun, without designating what spiritual things are meant; spiritual powers or forces is the best translation in the context) of evil, in the heavenlies.

The phrase "in the heavenlies" has appeared five times in Ephesians (1:3, 20, 2:6, 3:10; 6:12). The five verses that use this phrase say the following: the spiritual blessings God gives Christians are in the heavenlies with all spiritual blessings in Christ, Christ is seated at God's right hand in the heavenlies, Christians are now seated with Christ in the heavenlies, God's manifold wisdom is made known to rulers and authorities in the heavenlies, evil forces that oppose Christians are in the heavenlies. The word "heavenlies" is an adjective that functions as a noun (a substantive). The specific noun must be supplied based on context. Based on the various references in the verses cited, the heavenlies are a realm or a sphere. The heavenlies are not heaven; they are a spiritual realm. Note that evil powers are described as part of this realm.

6:13. The third imperative in this context is "to take" (*analambano*, receive, take up) the whole armor of God so you may be able (subjunctive, *dunamai*) to stand (*anthistemi*, stand against) in the evil day, and having done everything (*katergazomai*, accomplished, finished), to stand (*histemi*, cf. 6:11, in the sense of remaining standing, standing firm; cf. 6:14).

6:14-17. The imperative "stand" (*histemi*) is repeated to begin a new sentence, followed by four participles: having girded, having put on, having bound, and having taken up (vv. 14-16). The participles are related grammatically to the imperative. The participles are followed by another imperative in v. 17: receive. The participial verbs and the parts of the Christian armor deserve a brief explanation.

Having been girded with truth (there is no article in Greek, the abstract concept may be better translated truthfulness).

Having put on the breastplate of righteousness (*dikaiosune*), referring either to the righteousness of Christ or the righteousness that we have received through Christ.

Having bound your feet in readiness (preparation) of the gospel of peace. The subjective genitive would mean that the gospel of peace makes us ready. The objective genitive would mean that our feet are prepared to carry the gospel of peace.

Above all, having taken up the shield of faith with which you can extinguish all the flaming missiles of evil (or of the evil one).

6:17. The imperative and four participles of vv. 14-16 are followed by one more imperative in the context of the Christian armor. Receive (*dechomai*) the helmet of salvation and the sword of the Spirit which is the word (*rhema*) of God.

6:18-20. Contextually, it seems natural to make a literary break between v. 17 and v. 18, but the participle of v. 18 relates to the imperative (receive) of v. 17: praying always with all prayer and supplication. The repetition of Spirit is interesting and provides a connection. Spirit is anarthrous (without the article) and may be read as "in the Holy Spirit" or "in spirit." Numerous authors have noted the repeated use of "all" in v. 18. The focus on prayer is evident: praying always, with all kinds of prayer (*proseuche*) and supplication (*deesis*), with perseverance making supplication (*deesis*).

6:19-20. In vv. 19-20, Paul asks for prayers for him and his ministry in the gospel. His prayer request involves four things: to have the words (to be given words), to open his mouth boldly to proclaim the mystery of the gospel, to declare it boldly, to speak as he ought. These four items may be chiastic, with the first and last being parallel (words and speaking), and the second and third being parallel (to open his mouth boldly and to declare boldly). Mystery of the gospel probably refers to the same mystery as 1:9-10 and 3:2-6, that is, God's plan to bring together all people in Christ. Paul calls himself an ambassador (*presbeuo*, literally a senior, an old man, but figurative referring to a representative, a preacher) in chains.

Prayer and Evangelism
Pray to have the words needed
Pray to be bold in proclaiming the gospel
Pray to have the right words

6:21-24. The final greetings in Ephesians are brief in comparison to Paul's other letters. Ephesians and Colossians are often considered "sister letters" due to similar themes and wording. Here, vv. 21-22 are parallel to Col. 4:7-8, but in Colossians Paul adds a descriptive phrase concerning Tychicus: "fellow bond servant." Tychicus (Acts 20:4; Col. 4:7; Tit. 3:12, 2 Tim. 4:12) carried the letter. He would in addition give a report about Paul and his work, which was one of Paul's reasons for sending him (v. 22), to encourage the recipients.

6:23-24. The final salutation is typical. Incorruptible (*aphtharsia*) may also be translated unending, unchanging, genuine, or sincere.

CHAPTER SUMMARY

The way Christians submit to one another is not only demonstrated in the relationship of wives and husbands, it is also demonstrated in the relationship of children and parents, and in the relationship of slaves and masters. Have a submissive spirit, considering the wellbeing of the other, especially those of you who are empowered by the culture.

Finally, recognize that there is a spiritual battle at hand. God provides everything necessary. Therefore stand, being girded, having put on the breastplate, having bound your feet, having taken up the shield. Receive the helmet and the sword, praying always with all kinds of prayers and all kinds of supplications, with all perseverance. Please pray for my ministry.

I am sending you news about me and how things are here. Peace, love, faith, grace to those who love Christ Jesus with a never changing, unending love.

Introduction to Philippians

Philippians is difficult to outline, perhaps because it is such an informal and personal letter. Paul does not identify himself as an apostle in the salutation. Paul established a close relationship with this church despite his brief visit and rapid departure as narrated in Acts 16. Paul had a special place in his heart for this church, perhaps because it was the first church established on the second missionary journey as he and his companions worked to expand the gospel to new fields. This close relationship is reflected in the fact that he was helped in his missionary work with financial support this new church provided (Phil. 1:5, 7; 4:15). Receiving financial help does not seem to be Paul's usual practice, as he on other occasions mentions that he was providing his own living to preach the gospel freely without charge. Compare Phil. 4:16 where Paul mentions financial support received from Philippi with 1 Thess. 2:9 where he mentions working in Thessalonica so as not to burden the new believers. It appears that Paul worked at his occupation (tentmaking) during his stay in Thessalonica and that the money received from his secular work was supplemented by gifts from Philippi.

Philippians is counted among the Prison Epistles (so named because these letters were written while Paul was in prison). Paul's focus on the theme of "joy" is often mentioned in studies of the book. In the reading, analysis, and paragraphing, the student will want to seek out other themes. For example, the word "gospel" appears seven times in the first chapter. A reference to Jesus occurs 51 times (somewhat incredible in a book of only 104 verses).

The City

Paul and his companions came to the city of Philippi of Macedonia on the second missionary journey, as recorded in Acts 16. The city was located on the Ignatian Way, a major east-west Roman road. Philippi was named for Philip II of Macedon, the father of Alexander the Great. (The original

Thracian town was named Krenides.) The region became a Roman Province in 168 B.C. and became a Roman Colony in 31 B.C. (see Acts 16:12). This meant that the inhabitants of Philippi were citizens of Rome with numerous advantages. Paul refers to citizenship in Phil. 1:26 and to heavenly citizenship in Phil. 3:20, knowing that his readers would understand well the point concerning the responsibilities and the advantages of such citizenship status.

The Bible Context from Acts

On the second missionary journey, Paul concluded (Acts 16:6-10) that the so-called Macedonian call, received in a vision, was God's instruction to go westward from Troas to Macedonia. As a result, the gospel came to Philippi. We know from the text of Acts that Paul had with him Silas, Timothy, and Luke. Luke, as author of Acts, remains anonymous throughout the book of Acts, but his presence with Paul is indicated by the "we" passages in Acts. Luke came to Philippi with the traveling missionary group ("we") but apparently did not leave with them ("they"). The "we" sections of Acts end and begin again at Philippi. Later in Acts, Paul returned to Philippi on the third journey (Acts 20:1-3,6).

Author, Date, and Recipients

Author. That Paul is the author is stated in 1:1. That Paul is the author was generally accepted very early. There are many first-person pronouns in the letter, by which the author describes his own life, experience, and connection to Philippi. There are several quotes and allusions to Philippians in early extrabiblical Christian literature. Timothy was with Paul at the time of the writing and is mentioned in the salutation (see also 2:19-24, Paul was planning to send Timothy to visit the Philippians). Timothy worked with Paul in the spread of the gospel and may have served as a secretary (amanuensis).

Date. The date of this letter is linked to one of Paul's imprisonments—in Ephesus, Philippi, Caesarea, or Rome. A Roman imprisonment best fits the facts of Acts (also mentioned in the Marcionite prologue to Philippians). The best educated guess for the date of the writing of Philippians is Paul's first imprisonment in Rome in the early 60s. Philippians makes clear that Paul anticipated being released from prison so that he would be able to visit them (1:17-27; 2:24). References to the Roman soldiers and servants in Caesar's household also suggest Rome as a location, but the references are not conclusive as there could have been soldiers and servants in other Roman cities.

Here is a possible chronology of Paul's writings with locations and notations concerning their relationship to the book of Acts. Dates are approximate.

Book	Date	Place of Writing	Relationship to Acts
Galatians	50	Syrian Antioch	Acts 14:28; 15:2
1 Thessalonians	51	Corinth	Acts 18:5
2 Thessalonians	51	Corinth	
1 Corinthians	55	Ephesus	Acts 19:20
2 Corinthians	56	Macedonia	Acts 20:2
Romans	57	Corinth	Acts 20:3
Colossians	early 60s	Rome	Acts 28
Philemon	early 60s	Rome	Acts 28
Ephesians	early 60s	Rome	Acts 28
Philippians	early 60s	Rome	Acts 28
1 Timothy	63 (or later)	Macedonia	After Acts
Titus	63 ??		After Acts
2 Timothy	64-68	Rome	After Acts

Recipients. The salutation of the letter mentions the saints in Philippi, along with bishops and deacons. Apparently, the Philippian church was biblically organized within a few years of its establishment. There are approximately 10 years between the establishment of the Philippian church in Acts 16 and the date of the book.

Based on various biblical references, it appears that women may have had significant freedom in Macedonia. A group of women were worshiping by the river, we read of Lydia who is described as a businesswoman, women are mentioned as co-workers in the gospel (4:2-3), and women were also mentioned in Thessalonica (Acts 17:4, Thessalonica was also in Macedonia).

Purpose of the Letter

The letter is highly personal, and expectedly contains several personal references. Paul wants to update and assure the Philippians of his status. A short list of the personal references would include gratitude for the financial help extended, explanation of the situation with Epaphroditus, encouragement concerning the future of the gospel, encouragement against false teachings, encouragement in the midst of external pressures, and instructions about internal conflicts.

Paul also wants the Philippians to know of the past, present, and future advance of the gospel. With Paul in prison and his future uncertain, it may be that the Philippians were wondering about the future of the cause of Christ, a cause to which they had committed themselves and a cause in which they had participated financially in fellowship with Paul. What will happen to the gospel if Paul cannot continue traveling and preaching freely?

Paul wants to encourage the Philippians to continue faithfully in the gospel. This admonition begins in Chapter 1 and continues throughout the book. In Chapter 2, Paul sets forth a highly theological description of Jesus as an example to be followed in service and sacrifice. On the basis of these teachings, Paul calls the Philippians to Christian living, using a variety of illustrations and instructions—live as responsible citizens, fight for the gospel, unite, sacrifice, shine forth, cast off worthless things, seek to know Christ, hit the bulls-eye, forget the past and focus on the future, celebrate heavenly citizenship, depend on God, think positive thoughts. The careful student will be able to add to this list of illustrations and instructions.

General Outline of the Letter

It is difficult to outline Philippians due to the content and the personal nature of the letter. The book naturally divides into two parts, as do many of Paul's letters. These two parts are typically described as the doctrinal teaching and the practical application. In Philippians, the teaching part is identified as Chapters 1-2 and the practical part as Chapters 3-4. However, at times it seems that Paul's mind is overflowing with numerous things he wants to say to this church, so that the progression of thought is difficult to outline. The challenge of outlining the letter will become clearer in the study of the four brief chapters.

The major literary units that can be identified include the following, although some studies identify smaller textual units.

1:1-2	salutation
1:3-11	prayer
1:12-26	explanation of personal situation as it relates to the gospel
1:27-2:4	live out the gospel, instructions based on what has been presented
2:5-11	early Christian hymn, Christological section
2:12-18	live out the example of Christ, instructions based on what has been presented
2:19-30	personal section, Paul's plans regarding Philippi, Timothy, and Epaphroditus
3:1-21	stand firm in Christ, against false ideas
4:1-9	admonitions to unity, joy, certain attitudes
4:10-20	personal section, gratitude for their help
4:21-23	closing

Philippians 1

[Note: it is suggested that the student read the introductory materials on pages 3-8 of this guide before beginning any individual preparatory reading and analysis.]

CONTENT

The outlines and paragraphing included in the Content section of each chapter are merely suggestions or guides. The student is encouraged to identify the paragraphs, and the subsections within each paragraph, to assist in personal study. The division of the biblical text into paragraphs is fairly standard in modern translations. I have treated 1:12-26 as a paragraph based on the quasi-parenthetical use of the idea of progress.

Outline of the Chapter
1:1-2, salutation and greetings
1:3-11, prayer for the Philippians
1:12-26, progress of the gospel
1:27-31, living according to the gospel

STUDY HELPS

1:1-2. The salutation is typically Pauline. Timothy is included in the greeting although we have little biblical information concerning his presence with Paul during the Roman imprisonment. It may be that Timothy was able to travel between Ephesus (cf. 1 Timothy and 2 Timothy) and Rome periodically. Paul sent Timothy to help the church at Philippi (2:19-24). A study tracing Timothy's travels in support of the gospel is an interesting study, but beyond the scope of this study guide.

Bondservants (*doulos*, literally slaves) of Christ Jesus probably does not refer to physical imprisonment, but to their commitment as slaves of Christ (compare a similar reference in Eph. 4:1). Paul does not identify himself as an apostle, perhaps due to the personal nature of the book and the closeness of the relationship he had with the Philippian church. Paul's apostleship was not primarily in view and he does not need to mention his apostleship to have authority in the Philippian church. He writes from the context of a personal relationship with the recipients. For further study, look at Acts 16:1-17:14; 18:5-19:22; 20:4; Gal. 1:1; Rom. 16:21; 1 Cor. 4:17, 16:10; 2 Cor. 1:1,19; Phil. 1:1, 2:19-24; Philm. 4; and the salutations in 1 Timothy and 2 Timothy.

The reference to the saints (*hagios*) in Philippi is a usual way of describing Christians. God's people are holy "in Christ Jesus." Paul includes the overseers (*episkopos*, bishops) and deacons (*diakonos*) in the greeting. In the New Testament, the words pastor, elder, and bishop all refer to the same group of leaders in the local church (Acts 20:17,28; 1 Pet. 5:1-4; cf. Tit. 1:5,7). Bishop (*episkopos*, overseer) had a Greek background; elder (*presbuteros*) had a Jewish background. The Philippian church had apparently developed its leadership according to the model described in other parts of the New Testament, despite Paul's general absence from Philippi. Perhaps Luke had been a part of the leadership development in this church. (The likelihood that Luke stayed in Philippi when the rest of the missionary team went on to Thessalonica is explained in the Introduction, p. 70). Deacon is a general word for servant or minister, but was used in a more official sense in Ephesus (cf. 1 Tim. 3:8ff) and in Philippi. The biblical text supports these two leadership functions in the local church, although women servants are mentioned in 1 Tim. 3:11, possibly a reference to the widows' role (see my comments on 1 Timothy 3 in the *Bible Study Guide: Pastoral Letters*). While the roles of bishops and deacons were originally tasks or works that focused on service, in the early history of the church these quickly became titles and offices in a ecclesiastical hierarchy with a focus on power.

Grace and peace are usual in the salutations of Paul's letters.

1:3-11. The Greek letter form typically opened with a prayer, and Paul follows the same pattern. I identify 1:3-8 as Paul's prayer of thanksgiving for the Philippian church and 1:9-11 as his prayer for their maturity. In this view, v. 8 is transitional between the two prayers, but it is also possible to speak of one prayer of Paul with two different subjects.

1:3-8. Paul often mentions in his letters that he is praying for the churches to which he writes. The reference to joy introduces a theme that echoes through the book (*chara*, 1:4, 25; 2:2, 29; 4:1; *chairo*, 1:18; 2:17, 18, 28; 3:1; 4:4, 10; *sunchairo*, 2:17, 18; *chairo* and *sunchairo* used together, 2:17, 18).

1:5. Paul is grateful for their fellowship (*koinonia*, sharing, participation, help) in the gospel. This probably refers to their financial help (see Phil. 4:15; cf. Rom. 12:13; 15:26; 2 Cor. 9:13; Gal. 6:6; 1 Tim. 6:18, where *koinonia* is an idiom that refers to financial help). This financial help is described in 4:10, 14-18.

1:6. "I am confident." Paul writes with confidence about God's desire for the continued work of the Philippian church. Confidence is translated from a word that means to be persuaded, thus to be certain.

"He who began a good work in you...." The subject of this phrase is not stated but, in the context, the reference is to God. God initiates his work in human beings and he is the one who will complete (perfect) it. The future tense ("he will complete it") again indicates certainty. This is not primarily an eschatological passage, but it does show the tension between the "already" and the "not yet" of the Christian life. "Until the day of Christ Jesus" is most likely a reference to Jesus' coming (see parallels in 1:10 and 2:16).

1:7-8. These verses reflect the close relationship between Paul and the Philippians. They shared (were partakers together) of the grace of God. In this verse, we encounter the first of several references to the gospel in the first chapter. "The defense and confirmation of the gospel" includes terms that were used to describe a legal defense. Defense (*apologia*) and confirmation (*bebaiosis*, a legal guarantee) suggest that Paul was presenting the gospel boldly, whether defending it or actively advancing its proclamation.

The phrase, "You share together with me," uses the word *koinonia* (fellowship with, 2:1; 3:10; 4:14, 16 are related passages). Paul in this book uses a number of compound words that begin with "*sun*." These words show how Christians share together in the work of the gospel. Examples include fellowship with, partakers with (1:7, 4:14), striving together (*sun-athlountes*) with the meaning of working together or cooperating (1:27), of the same mind (literally, souls together) (2:2), rejoicing together (2:17-18), working together, fellow workers (2:25, 4:3), soldiers together, fellow soldiers (2:25), formed together, becoming like him (3:10), and imitating together, join in imitating me (3:17).

Paul closes the first part of the prayer by mentioning the special relationship he had with the Philippians (v. 8).

1:9-11. Having described various aspects of his past relationship with the Philippians in vv. 3-8, Paul now turns to his prayer for their future. These three verses are one sentence in Greek: a prayer for abounding love in knowledge and discernment, giving the ability to understand what is best, being filled with the fruit of righteousness to be ready for the day of Christ.

"That your love may abound" is present active subjunctive expressing hope for continued growth. Abound (*perisseuo*) means to be filled to overflowing. Knowledge (*epignosis*) is an intensified form from *gnosis*: full knowledge, real knowledge, insight. Discernment (*aesthesis*) is understanding and good judgment.

To approve (*dokimazo*) means to test, often referring to metals or coins. It often meant to approve on the basis of the testing. In this context, it means to know by testing, and thus to approve, what is best (*diaphero*, literally, the things that carry through). *Diaphero* can be translated "things that differ," carrying the idea of making a distinction. In the context, the idea refers to things that last or remain, thus excellent things. A possible translation would be: "the things that are really important or of real value" (cf. Rom. 2:18 where the same word is used). The text suggests the ability to understand priorities and to choose what is best. The result is a Christian who is sincere. "Sincere" translates an interesting Greek word that combines sunshine and judgment, literally "to test in the light," leading to the idea (and translation) of being free from impurity. The Christian is also blameless (*aproskopos*), not causing offense or stumbling in others. Day of Christ refers to Jesus' return.

"Having been filled" (present passive participle) connects to and depends on the preceding thought, describing what had happened previously to make the Christian sincere and blameless until the day of Christ. The fruit borne in the Christian life is righteousness, a righteousness that is possible only through Jesus Christ. The result is to the glory and praise of God (cf. Eph. 1:6, 12, 14).

1:12-26. I treat this extended section as a single literary unit on the basis of the parenthetical references to progress. The progress of the gospel (v. 12) leads to progress and joy in the faith for the Philippians (vv. 25-26).

The Gospel in Philippians 1

1:5, partners in the gospel

1:7, defend and confirm the gospel

1:12, advance the gospel

1:13, the gospel (it) has become known

1:16, defend the gospel

1:27, live worthy of the gospel

1:27, strive for the gospel

"I want you to know...." Perhaps the Philippians had asked Paul some questions through Epaphroditus. The Philippian church had participated with the gospel from the beginning. With Paul in prison, the future perhaps appeared uncertain. What would happen to the gospel if Paul died in prison? What would happen without the efforts of Paul in the churches? Such questions would be normal in the first century context in which the letter was written. Paul wanted to assure the Philippians with regard to the gospel and the future. The historical context of this section must guide understanding.

1:12-14. Paul shares good news. His situation in prison is helping the gospel go forward. The guards and everyone else have become aware that he is imprisoned for Christ. Despite the fact that such circumstances could work against the gospel, God is always at work regardless of our good or bad circumstances. God works in mysterious ways, in Paul's ministry and in our lives today. The progress (*prokope*, advancement) of the gospel carries the idea of trailblazing or following a difficult path. The gospel was progressing among the guards and throughout the palace, among those who are in places that were formerly considered enemy territory. The gospel was progressing because other preachers were being encouraged to preach the word of God more boldly as a result of Paul's experiences.

1:15-18. Paul mentions that some preachers of Christ operate from envy, but others from good will and love. Who the envious preachers are has been widely debated. Most likely the message was right but the motives were wrong, because of their attitude toward Paul. Perhaps they were leaders who had been displaced or had lost some of their former power and prestige with Paul's presence. The same results can be seen in churches today—poor attitudes, jealousy, the party-spirit, divisiveness.

1:16-18. I have been put in this place (*keimai*, set, appointed) for the defense of the gospel. The verb was used of putting a soldier on watch. Defense (*apologia*) is repeated from v. 7. The situation is described again: some proclaim Christ out of selfish ambition (perhaps arrogance) and not from pure motives. The situation could have caused Paul concern. But for Paul, that Christ is proclaimed is cause for rejoicing, whether by pretenders or in truth. Preaching the gospel supersedes personal matters.

1:19-21. Paul rejoices because he believes the events he is describing will be the source of his deliverance (*soteria*, literally salvation). The word does not refer to spiritual salvation in Christ, but as the context shows, to Paul's deliverance from his situation. Paul believed he would be released (v. 22). His release would be possible through the prayers of the Philippians and the provision (*epichoregia*, something supplied or provided) of the Spirit.

Such is Paul's expectation and hope, believing that his confidence in God will be rewarded and that he will not feel shame for having been proved wrong in this expectation. He is therefore bold to speak, because his goal is that Christ will now and always be exalted in his body, whether in life or death. The Christian honors God by how he or she uses the physical body.

1:21. A well-known verse, frequently quoted, caps this sub-section. "To live is Christ, to die is gain." To live (present infinitive) is a continuous action. Death (aorist infinitive) is a one-time event. The reference here is to physical death, which for Paul meant being with Christ.

1:22-26. If I live (the first class condition is considered true), that will result in fruitful labor. Paul sees advantages in both options. If he had to make a choice, he does not know which choice he would make. Paul's words here along with other biblical and historical evidence suggest that Paul was released from prison sometime after he wrote the Prison Epistles.

1:23-24. Paul feels pressure (*sunecho*, pressed or held together tightly). He has the desire to depart to be with Christ, a much better option. But he also sees that it would be more helpful to the Philippians that he remains in the flesh (alive).

1:25-26. Paul expected to be released from prison, "I know I will remain and continue with you...." The results would be progress and joy in the faith for the Philippians. These two verses are one sentence in Greek. These two results introduce two major themes of the book. Their confidence and pride in Paul would be even more abundant when it was possible for him to come to them again.

1:27-30. The Christian is to live (present imperative, *politeuomai*, to live as a citizen) in a manner worthy of the gospel. These verses are one long sentence in Greek. Note the reference to the gospel—to live worthy of the gospel. Regardless of what happened to Paul, whether he was able personally to come to visit them or not, he would hear of their way of life. This lifestyle is described in a series of descriptive phrases:

- standing firm (present, active, indicative) in one spirit (in this context, likely referring to one commitment),
- of one mind (thinking alike),
- striving together (*sunathleo*, where you can see the root for our word athlete; in the verb *sunathleo*, one can also note the idea of teamwork) for the faith of the gospel (the faith, with the article, a reference to the body of Christian truth),
- not concerned because of the opponents.

The attitude of the Philippians would bear evidence that those who oppose Christ and Christianity are destined for destruction, while Christians will be saved by God. Saved, as in

v. 19, is likely a reference to physical salvation, in which case the destruction of the opponents may also be physical.

1:29-30. Christians have been called both to believe and to suffer for Christ. The fact that Paul was experiencing the conflict of faith and suffering was evidence that such was a reasonable expectation for the Philippians. In fact, in the New Testament the suffering of Christians is a given. Paul had been persecuted during his first visit to Philippi (Acts 16:22-24).

CHAPTER SUMMARY

Greetings to the saints in Philippi, and also to the bishops and deacons: grace and peace.

I want you to know how thankful I am for your past life—especially how you have shared in the work of the gospel. God made that possible, and he will keep on doing the work he has begun until Jesus comes again. We have shared life, and I long for you and have you in my heart, regardless of my circumstances. I also pray about your future, so you will grow in love and knowledge and insight, choosing the things of greatest value, always prepared for the day of Christ, bearing fruit in Christ.

Now concerning my imprisonment and the gospel, I want you to know that my time in prison has worked to advance the gospel. The whole palace is hearing the gospel, and more and more brothers are speaking fearlessly. Not all have pure motives, but the gospel is being preached. I think all of this will turn out so that I am released, but regardless of what happens, my goal is to exalt Christ. Living is Christ, dying is gain. Living means fruitful work, but dying would mean being with Christ. I will remain and you will continue to progress in the faith.

It is imperative that you live in a manner consistent with the gospel. Be firm, stand together, contend for the gospel, don't pay attention to the opponents. You have been blessed, not only to believe in him but also to suffer for him, the very same thing that has happened to me.

Philippians 2

[Note: it is suggested that the student read the introductory materials on pages 3-8 of this guide before beginning any individual preparatory reading and analysis.]

CONTENT
The paragraphing included in the Content section of each chapter provides suggestions or guides. The student is encouraged to identify the paragraphs and subsections within each paragraph to assist in his or her own study. The division of the biblical text into paragraphs is fairly standardized in modern translations.

Outline of the Chapter
2:1-11, preserve unity by developing the mind of Christ and imitating the humility of Christ
2:12-18, lights in the world
2:19-30, information about Timothy and Epaphroditus

Observations about the Content of the Chapter
      The theme of unity is often overlooked in the Philippian letter.
      The text of 2:6-11 is likely an early Christian hymn.
      The personal nature of the letter is shown in the extended explanation about Timothy and Epaphroditus.

STUDY HELPS
2:1-4. This is one sentence in the Greek text, with four first class conditional statements (assumed to be true). The first class condition functions here rhetorically: since there is…. "If there is….," and there is!
      If there is encouragement in Christ (*paraklesis*, encouragement, often translated as comfort or exhortation, possibly meaning stimulation or motivation).

If there is any comfort (*paramuthion*) of love. The relationship between comfort and love is that love is comforting (New English Translation, NET, the comfort provided by love).

If there is fellowship (*koinonia*, sharing) of the Spirit (compare 2 Cor. 13:14), and there is! Spirit does not have the definite article. While this verse may refer to the Holy Spirit, it may refer to the connection of human spirits, that is, spiritual fellowship. Is Paul ever purposefully ambiguous?

If there is affection (literally, bowels, referring to the idea that the abdomen was thought to be the seat of emotions) and mercy (*oiktirmos*). The meanings overlap in several of the words in 2:1.

2:2. "Fulfill my joy, thinking the same things, with the same love, like-minded, thinking with one purpose." The Philippians are urged to complete Paul's joy by their actions toward one another. The focus is on unity, demonstrated by "one another" Christianity. Thinking (*phroneo*) is used twice in this verse, which I have reflected in my translation above (for other uses of this Greek word in the book, see 1:7; 2:5; 3:15, 19; 4:2, 10). The primary translation question is how to translate the first phrase which has a subjunctive verb (in order to think the same things). A common approach is to consider the phrase as epexegetical (added words to explain what precedes it). "Complete my joy by being of the same mind" (English Standard Version, ESV), or "complete my joy and be of the same mind" (NET). This gives an imperatival force to both verbs—complete my joy and think the same things, which in turn gives an imperatival force to the participles that follow.

How to accomplish this is then set forth with a series of four present participles in 2:2-4—having the same love, like-minded ones thinking with one purpose, regarding others as better than self, looking out for the things of others. Clustered around these verbal forms are several explanatory phrases. A somewhat awkward but fairly literal translation is this: "Having (*echo*) the same love, like-minded ones thinking (*phroneo*) with one purpose, no one according to strife or vanity but in humility considering (*hegeomai*) others better than self, each one not his own things looking after (*skopeo*) but the things of others."

Paul is likely anticipating the problems that have arisen in the Philippian church due to strife and pride (see 4:2-3). Humility was not a virtue in the Roman world. As Paul concludes the letter, he includes similar concepts in 4:8-9.

> *"who existing in the form of God did not think equality with God a thing to be seized for self, but he emptied himself, taking the form of a servant, being in likeness as a human being, and being found in appearance as a man, he humbled himself, becoming obedient unto death, death on a cross."* Phil. 2:6-8

2:5-11. Have the same attitude (present active imperative) repeats the word "think" (*phroneo*). Think like Christ. Have in yourselves what was also in Christ. Christ-like actions begin with Christ-like thinking.

2:6. This verse introduces a poetic section (2:6-11) that was likely a hymn quoted by Paul. Several words in this section are not found elsewhere in Paul's writings. Christians are to imitate Christ in thought, in humility, in sacrifice, and in service. Christ was self-abasing and self-giving.

2:6-11. A good way to explain the structure of this section is to note the focus on Jesus' nature and actions, followed by a focus on God the Father's actions. Jesus, preexisting in divine nature, became incarnate in human form, and humbly sacrificially died on a cross. God the Father exalted him, with universal confession of his name and lordship over all. Several great theological truths are presented in this section.

- Jesus is truly God (divine in essence, *morphe*).
- Jesus is truly human (in form, *schema*).
- He took the essence (*morphe*) of a servant and the likeness (*homoioma*) of humanity.
- Jesus shared human nature and obediently went to the cross.
- The result is that God exalted him as truly worthy of worship, making him Lord of all, and this by the will of God and to the glory of God.

Let us consider these one at a time in detail.

<u>Jesus is truly God</u>. The first description of Jesus is this phrase: "who in the form of God being." This is a present tense verb form in a series of aorist (past tense) forms. The point is the pre-existence of Jesus with divine essence, that Jesus was already existing. Jesus did not come into existence in the Incarnation. Jesus' pre-existence is an evidence of his deity. Jesus did not consider being equal with God something to be seized for himself. The present infinitive (to be) I have translated with the present participle (being). Jesus always exists (existed, exists, will exist) with the essence of God and in equality with God (Deity, but in the context usually understood as a reference to God the Father). Jesus is fully God. Grasped (seized) is from the Greek verb *harpazo*. (*Harpazo* has three basic dimensions or uses—something unexpected or sudden, something done with much force, and something done for personal gain. See my comments on 1 Thess. 4:13-18 where *harpazo* means unexpectedly. In the context of Philippians 2, it means to seize for personal gain.)

<u>Jesus became truly human</u>. Literally, he emptied himself. He chose to come to earth and live as a human being. He voluntarily humbled himself in the limitations of human existence. A question that has been long-debated is the nature of Jesus in the Incarnation. Was he half divine and half human? Was he all human with no divine essence? Is it possible to be 100% divine and 100% human at the same time? It is hard to understand how one gives up one's essence. Heb. 1:3 says Jesus has the exact character of God's essence, an apparent reference to his earthly existence. The best option is to say that Jesus did not cast off his divine nature in his Incarnation, but that he accepted human nature. With a human nature, he was tempted (Matthew 4; Luke 4), tested (John 4), fearful (Luke 22, in Gethsemane), and obedient (Heb. 5:8-9). Note these facts from Phil. 2:6-11: he left eternity and existence with God the Father, he was humbled so that he could later be exalted, his name (nature) was like other human beings so that he could receive a name above all, he lived "not as Lord" so that he could be declared Lord of all. He fully experienced our humanity, and being divine in essence, he became the perfect mediator, being a faithful and merciful high priest (Heb. 2:17-18).

He took the essence of a servant and the likeness of humanity. He took the form (*morphe*) of a servant (*doulos*, slave) is a phrase exactly parallel to the "form of God" in v. 6. To become a slave is to give up personal privilege and choose to serve. Here the emphasis is on the one-time event of Jesus' Incarnation (aorist tense forms), not on his continuing existence (present tense forms). Jesus became fully human. "Likeness of humanity" may remind of the creation of human beings in the likeness of God (Gen. 1:26-27). This phrase, the "likeness of humanity," does not mean that Jesus participated in human sinfulness. The fact that Jesus could take human likeness or human nature without experiencing fallenness and sin shows the fallacy of a commonly-accepted theology that sees human nature as sinful. Having human nature does not demand sin; babies are not born in sin simply because they are human beings. Sin enters the human experience when human beings share the decision of Adam to rebel against God. (See my comments on Romans 5 for more on this topic. Also see Rom. 8:3; 1 Cor. 5;21; Heb. 4:15-16; 1 Pet. 2:22.)

Jesus shared human nature and obediently went to the cross (v. 7-8). The text says Jesus was in the essence of a servant, likeness of men, and appearance (*schema*) as a man. *Morphe* was usually understood to refer to the inner unchanging forms and essence; *schema* was usually understood to refer to the outward changing forms that were not dependent on essence. The point is that Jesus' essence was a divine servant, in human likeness, with the outward form of a man. These three descriptors combine in the statement that he humbled himself becoming obedient to the point of death on the cross (aorist verb forms).

God exalted him, giving him a name above all, making him Lord of all, and this by the will of God and to the glory of God (vv. 9-11). It is important to note that this hymn does not present two Christologies. On the basis of what has been said about Jesus' preexistence as Deity with the inner essence of God, and his Incarnation with the inner essence of a slave, with human likeness and outward human form—therefore, God has acted to exalt him. God also gave (*charizomai*) him a name above every name, the name of Lord.

Every knee will bow at the name of Jesus. Every tongue will confess; one day everyone will acknowledge that Jesus is in fact Lord. In this way, God receives the glory he desires and deserves. All of this is according to the will of God.

2:12-18. When the Philippians live in imitation of Jesus, with the mind or attitude of Christ, they will be lights in the world.

2:12-13. These two verses are one sentence in Greek. Thus (so then) points back to the previous section. "My beloved ones" reflects Paul's concern for this church, although the phrase is not unusual in Paul's writings (see Rom. 12:19; 16:8,9,12; 1 Cor. 4:14,17; 10:14; 15:58; 2 Cor. 7:1; 12:19; Eph. 6:21; Phil. 4:1; Col. 4:7,9,14; 1 Tim. 6:2; 2 Tim. 1:2; Philm. 1,2,16).

Paul describes them as obedient in the past whether he has been present or absent, and encourages them to continue in the same way, working out their salvation with fear (*phobos*, awe) and trembling (*tromos*, reverence). "Work out" can refer to solving a mathematical problem. The compound form (*katergazomai*, finish, fashion, bring to an end) does not deny the sovereignty of God in salvation and does not demand meritorious actions that result in salvation. The mystery of God's plan for salvation, extended by grace and received by faith, will never be understood by insisting on a strict dichotomy. (See my comments on Eph. 2:8-10). Paul clearly affirms both that God is at work (*energeo*, working in you), and that his work produces desire and effort in believers, according to his will. The use of the plural forms (you, your) in a letter written to a group of believers should not be interpreted to mean that these verses have no individual application.

2:14-18. This section begins with another long sentence (vv. 14-16). The admonition about grumbling and arguing possibly reflects the disunity and problems in Philippi. There were problems with some preachers (1:14-17), possible problems within the church (1:27-2:4), a need for humility and sacrifice (2:5-11), false teachers (3:2), and women in conflict (4:2-3). Here is a summary of the message in 2:14-16: Living without grumbling shows that the Christian is pure, blameless, without blemish, unpolluted by the surrounding worldly context, capable of shining as a light in the world. This is done by holding tightly to the word of God, and in the case of the Philippians, will result in glory for Paul in the day of Christ, knowing that he did not run or work in vain.

A believer must make choices. A believer chooses salvation; a believer must choose life and lifestyle. Blameless (*amemptos*) means without defect, a word used frequently to describe God's people. Pure (*akeraios*, innocent, spotless) refers to moral purity. Without blemish (*amometos*) may be translated without blame. The context in which believers live is crooked (*skolios*) and distorted (from *diastrepho*, turned away). The world has no interest in the word of God and does not measure up to its standard. In the midst of such a world, believers shine as lights (*phoster*, giving illumination) in the world. When Jesus said that Christians are the light of the world, he used different words but communicated the same idea. Being a light in the world is possible when one holds tightly or holds forth (*epecho*) the word of life. Note the two possible meanings of this verb: to hold on to firmly, or to hold forth or extend.

The Philippians' success in being lights and holding forth the word will be a cause of rejoicing for Paul in the day of Christ, referring to the coming of Christ. Paul will rejoice because he will know that his labors have produced fruit (were not in vain). Verses 17 and 18 have four references to rejoicing. Paul is being offered as a sacrifice for the development of the faith of the Philippians, a faith that is evidenced by sacrifice and service. Paul's sacrifice does not refer to his impending death. He has earlier expressed confidence in his release (1:25).

2:19-30. In this final section of the chapter, Paul explains his plans to send Timothy and Epaphroditus to the Philippians. These two helpers serve as models of ministry. Paul plans to send Timothy so that the Philippians will know Paul's status and so Paul can receive news of them. Paul anticipates that this will occur before he sends the letter, and that the letter will serve as explanation after-the-fact of what Paul has done. Then Paul plans to send Epaphroditus, possibly using Epaphroditus as the carrier of the letter. The description Paul gives of the situation of Epaphroditus will serve as explanation when the Philippians receive the letter.

2:19-24. Concerning Timothy, Paul says he hopes to send him soon. One of Paul's purposes was to receive news of the Philippians. Paul's description of Timothy presents a challenge to every Christian and to every minister: "I have no one else who shares such a like-spirit that is genuinely concerned for your welfare." It is not clear to whom Paul refers in v. 21, but the point is that people who share Timothy's concern for others are few, and that the typical attitude of Christians, and even ministers, is to look out for their own interests more than those things that advance the cause of Jesus Christ. Paul may be referring to the jealous preachers or the false teachers described in other parts of the book. Self-interest is an ever-present threat, and the modern church has not escaped the tendency to put the things of others and things of God in second place.

Timothy had shown his value (*dokime*, testing) by his past service, serving with Paul, as a child with a father, on behalf of the gospel. Paul was perhaps expecting some news about his legal case, and upon receiving the update, he planned to send Timothy to the Philippians with the news, and to receive news about them upon Timothy's return. Further, Paul himself hoped to be able to visit the Philippians soon. This is sometimes cited as evidence for dating Philippians as the last of the Prison Epistles.

2:25-30. Concerning Epaphroditus, the key to understanding this section is to recognize the epistolary aorist tenses so that Paul places himself in the position of the recipients of the letter and anticipates their reception of the letter in these verses. Another way to describe this technique is to say that Paul writes about these things as if they have already occurred.

With this understanding, we can summarize Paul's message. "I considered it necessary to send Epaphroditus, brother, fellow worker and fellow soldier to me, your representative (*apostolos*, used in non-technical sense) to me and your minister to my needs. I wanted to send him because he was longing for you and was distressed when you learned that he was sick. He was sick to the point of death, but God was merciful to him, and to me so that I did not have sorrow piled on top of sorrow.

Therefore, I am still eager to send him, and even more eager, so you can rejoice when you see him and I will no longer be anxious. Receive him, honor him and those like him, because he almost died because of his commitment to Christ's work. He risked his life to complete what was lacking in your ministry to me."

We know little about Epaphroditus. Epaphras is perhaps an abbreviated form of the name, but the Epaphras we know in the Bible is not the same person (cf. Col. 1:7; 4:12; Philm. 23). It appears that Epaphroditus was charged with delivering a financial gift to Paul in prison, a task that had brought him risk of life and life-threatening sickness. The "risk of life" probably refers to the life-threatening illness. Against the backdrop of modern-day faith healers, it is important and interesting to note how often in Scripture healing was not possible or the gift of healing was not used. Is the lack of healing always the result of lack of faith? The determining factor is not faith, but God's will. The word translated as "life" is *psuche*. The context determines meaning; the passage refers to the possible loss of life, not soul. The New Testament usage of the words for body, soul, and spirit at times seems inconsistent and is difficult to discern. Epaphroditus went to Paul in prison to help the Philippians accomplish what they had not had the opportunity to do. The idea of deficiency may sound negative, but it was simply an effort to do on behalf of the Philippians what they themselves could not do.

CHAPTER SUMMARY

The blessings that are available in Christ are more than sufficient reason for living in accord with the gospel, casting off every tendency toward self-centeredness and self-concern, and being concerned with the well-being of others. In fact, the gospel through Jesus and the Spirit calls us to mercy, love, humility, like-mindedness, and changed thinking. This will bring unity, including unity in purpose.

There is no better example of this changed thinking than Jesus himself. He gave up everything that might have been seen as of personal value or gain in order to become like us, he humbled himself so that he could look out for our best interests.

As a result, God exalted him so that it is evident to all that He is Lord.

You must diligently try to understand how to resolve personal conflicts and similar problems, just as God is energizing you and giving you the power and the desire to do everything possible to seek his will. When you do this with a Christlike spirit and with pure lives in a corrupted world, you will be genuine lights to the world. You will never be able to do this successfully unless you hang on tightly to the word of God and help others see that word. A part of my desire for you is selfish, because your faithfulness in imitating Jesus will make my service worthwhile, knowing that I have not labored in vain. In this we can rejoice together, I for you and you for me.

I want to update you about Timothy and Epaphroditus. First, I plan to send Timothy soon in order to find out firsthand how you are doing, and he will also deliver news about me to you. Timothy is exactly the right person for this task, he is concerned about you and he has faithfully served in the gospel. (When we see how my case is going to be resolved, I believe I will be able to come to you soon as well.)

Second, I consider it a necessity to send Epaphroditus to you. He has been helpful to me as your representative. He misses you and has been concerned about how you would receive the news of his illness. You know that he was so sick he almost died, so I am even more eager to send him. When he arrives, welcome him and honor him.

Philippians 3

[Note: it is suggested that the student read the introductory materials on pages 3-8 of this guide before beginning any individual preparatory reading and analysis.]

CONTENT

The outlines and paragraphing included in the Content section of each chapter are only suggestions or guides. The student is encouraged to identify the paragraphs, and subsections within each paragraph, to assist in his or her own study. The division of the biblical text into paragraphs is fairly standard in modern translations.

I have maintained the chapter division. Some would place 3:1 with the last paragraph of Chapter 2.

Outline of the Chapter
3:1-11, the true righteousness that is in Christ
3:12-16, pressing toward the mark
3:17-21, heavenly citizenship

STUDY HELPS

3:1-11. Paul addresses several matters in this extended paragraph. An introductory verse is followed by a warning against the Judaizing teachers. The warning is based on Paul's own experience in Judaism (vv. 2-6). Paul then sets forth that which he has come to recognize as genuine gain and of true value in Christ Jesus (vv. 7-11).

3:1. "Finally," *(loipon)* is literally, "for the rest." This is a common way to transition to a new subject, but it often occurs near the end of a letter (cf. 2 Cor. 13:11; Eph. 6:10; 1 Thess. 4:8; 2 Thess. 3:1). "Rejoice in the Lord" repeats a theme that appears frequently in the letter. Paul recognizes that he is repeating certain matters. The reference may be to a previous letter that is unknown to us, or it could anticipate the mention of the opponents, a topic he has previously addressed in the letter.

3:2-6. "Look out for" (present active imperative) is repeated three times. The Gentiles were sometimes called dogs by the Jews. Here Paul reverses that usage, referring to the false teachers, apparently Jewish teachers, as dogs. These false teachers held forth a false circumcision. In the insistence of the Judaizers that Gentiles also be circumcised (Acts 15; Gal. 5:2-3, 12), they were teaching that one could not be a Christian without becoming Jewish. Circumcision was a necessity for becoming a proselyte Jew. The insistence of some Jews on circumcision for every Christian is an evidence of how closely connected were the two faith systems during the early decades of Christianity, especially up to the destruction of the temple and the Jewish system in A.D. 70.

3:3. Paul writes that Christians are the circumcision, that is, spiritual Israel (cf. Gal. 6:16; Romans 9-11). "True" does not appear in the Greek text but is added in translation to make clearer Paul's meaning. That Christians are God's people is supported by three present active participles: worshipping in the Spirit of God, glorying (*kauchaomai*) in Christ, not putting confidence (*peitho*) in the flesh. Glory is sometimes translated as rejoice, boast, exalt, be confident, be proud. *Peitho* can be translated as rely, trust, yield, be persuaded by, obey. In contrast to Jews who put much confidence in their physical circumcision, even when it was not accompanied by heart commitment, Paul describes the Christians who are spiritual Israel as not measuring life by such external standards, even though he himself would measure up pretty well in consideration of his past life in Judaism.

3:4-6. If someone wants to put confidence in the flesh (first class condition is assumed to be true), Paul says that no one would have more reason to do that than he. Paul's Jewish credentials were virtually unequaled: circumcised; Israelite through and through; Benjaminite and thus of the same tribe as King Saul and from one of the faithful tribes that stayed with Judah in the south in the division into northern and southern kingdoms; a Hebrew of the Hebrews—perhaps of pure descent or perhaps a reference to his understanding of the language as a student of the Old Testament. Concerning the law, a Pharisee keeping every detail of the law, a persecutor of the church, a keeper of the law doing everything he could within his understanding of God's will.

3:7-11. Paul now values none of the things that he formerly considered so important (*kerdos*, gain), the things that the Judaizing teachers are still focused on. He is willing to let go of such things, to count (*hegeomai*) them as loss (*zemia*) because of Christ. Note the continued interaction of three concepts in this section: what Paul thinks about certain things, what is gained, what is lost.

    3:8-11. These verses are one extended sentence in Greek. Paul repeats the verb (*hegeomai*): I count everything to be loss (*zemia*) because of the excellency of the knowledge of Christ Jesus my Lord…. To know someone suggests personal relationship, not just the accumulation of facts about another person. In English, we make the distinction with "to know" and "to know about." Paul is describing the importance of knowing Jesus, not just knowing about Jesus. When we come to know Jesus, we can trust him and live obediently for him.

    …for whom I lost (*zemioo*) all things, and I count (*hegeomai*) them to be rubbish (*skubalon*, literally what is thrown to the dogs, refuse, dung) in order than I might gain (*kerdaino*) Christ. Paul also used the word "gain" in 1:21.

    3:9. …and be found in him. This is the second of two subjunctives: that I might gain, that I might be found. Paul frequently mentions the importance of being "in him" or "in Christ." To be in Christ is to reject the personal righteousness that comes through keeping the law. In Greek, righteousness and justification are not two words, but are translations of the same Greek word, with the translation depending on the context. Here, I am using righteousness as the translation since it fits the context.

    Righteousness before God is not possible through law-keeping, whether of the Old Law or of any legal system. To be righteous (justified) in God's sight is possible only through faith in Christ, a righteousness from God that is based on faith. The phrase, faith in Christ, raises again the question concerning the relationship of these two nouns that are connected with the genitive case. Is Christ the object of faith or the subject of faith? It is easy to read the phrase as an objective genitive, Christ is the object of our faith in him. But in Greek, it is equally easy to read the phrase as a subjective genitive so that Christ's faith (faithfulness) is the basis of our justification. Both readings present biblical truth. Our righteousness is possible because of Christ's faithfulness in doing God's will. Our righteousness depends on our faith response to Christ. In either case, this righteousness is from God.

3:10-11. The result Paul is seeking is "to know him, and the power of his resurrection, the fellowship of his sufferings, to be like him in his death, to attain (*katantao*, arrive at) the resurrection from the dead." "To know him" is repeated from v. 8. "The power of his resurrection" may mean that Paul wants to know or experience in his own life the power that resurrected Jesus (cf. Eph. 1:19-20), or it may refer to the resurrected, changed life that believers experience in Christ. "The fellowship (*koinonia*) of his sufferings" means that Paul was willing to undergo suffering. "Being conformed (*summorphoo*) to his death" reminds of the use of *morphe* in 2:6-9. This may refer to Paul's willingness to die for the cause of Christ, but it can also mean that all Christians are dead to sin and alive to God (Rom. 6:1-11; Gal. 2:20).

"To arrive at the resurrection of the dead" requires knowing Christ, experiencing the power of his resurrection, the sharing of his suffering, and the likeness of his death. In v. 11, the word for resurrection is compounded (*exanastasis*, in comparison to the more common *anastasis*). This is the only use of this compound form in the New Testament. The idea may be that in some way the ultimate resurrection from the dead is "out of" the power of Christ's resurrection in the Christian's daily life. The Christian experiences the resurrected life in Christ

---

The Christian wants....

To know Christ

To experience the power of his resurrection

To share in his sufferings

To be like him in his death

To attain resurrection from the dead

after baptism (Rom. 6:1-6) but also anticipates the final resurrection. This is a good example of the "already-not yet" tension of Christian salvation.

3:12-16. None of what Paul has written should be understood to suggest that he has already obtained (*lambano*, receive) these things, or that he has been perfected (*teleioo*, perfect passive indicative). *Teleioo* can mean complete, mature, fully able or fully equipped. The major point to be remembered is that in the New Testament, the word "perfect" with its various forms does not have the English connotation of sinlessness. Paul understood the tension between following Christ and anticipating future blessings. The present anticipates the future but does not always accurately represent the future. Suffering can lead to glory. Paul sought to arrive (*katantao*) but had not yet obtained it (*lambano*). The addition of "to have been righteous" in some manuscripts and translations is rejected in favor of the shorter textual reading.

     3:12-14. I pursue (*dioko*) in order to lay hold (*katalambano*, possess, find, obtain) that for which I was laid hold (*katalambano*) by Christ. But I have not yet laid hold of it (*katalambano*).

     Two participles precede Paul's description of his goal and show how he tries to accomplish the one thing of supreme importance. "Forgetting" (*epilanthanomai*) what is behind and "reaching forth" (*epekteinomai*) to what is ahead, with this goal in view (*skopos*), I pursue (*dioko*) the prize (*brabeion*) of the upward call of God in Christ Jesus.

     3:15-16. Therefore, let those of us who are mature (*teleios*, mature is a better translation than perfect in the context) think this. In the context, "this" must refer to some part of what Paul has just presented. To think (*phroneo*) refers to mental processes or reasoning, and also to attitude (remember the use of the same verb in 2:1-5). When (if, first class condition is assumed to be true) any of you think differently or have a different attitude, this also God will reveal to you. The interpretation of v. 15 is difficult. Paul affirms that he has received his message from God. It is therefore an authoritative message that should be accepted by those who are mature. Others who are less mature might have other thoughts or attitudes. Perhaps

Paul is referring to the opposing preachers, Christians with interpersonal conflicts, or false teachers. The interpretation of the last phrase may go two ways: perhaps Paul is saying that God will reveal truth to those who have other attitudes, or perhaps he is saying that God will reveal to the Christians who it is that is using other thinking.

3:16. The ultimate test of thinking is in the actions that result. "To what we have already attained (*phthano*, what is beforehand), let us conform (*stoicheo*)." A textual variant adds, "let us think according to the same standard or rule."

3:17-4:1. While an effort is being made to maintain the common chapter divisions, in this case it seems that 4:1 better belongs with the last part of Chapter 3.

3:17-21. Many of the older translations are difficult to understand. A fairly literal reading of the text is simple: "Be imitators of me and watch those walking in this way, just as you have us as an example." There are two imperatives in v. 17 —be imitators and watch.

3:18. Because many walk (live), about whom I told you many times, and now weeping I tell you, they are enemies of the cross of Christ. Who these enemies are is not clear. Perhaps they are the false teachers, but the list of sins that follows suggests the possibility that some Christians at Philippi were returning to Greek philosophies or pagan lifestyles.

3:19. The description of the "enemies" of v. 18 continues. "Whose end is destruction, whose god is their appetite (*koilia*, literally stomach, but figuratively meaning appetite) and the glory of their shame, who think about (*phroneo*) earthly or worldly things." Some who were formerly Christians have become enemies and will be lost. They glory in shameful things.

3:20-21. The citizenship of Christians is in heaven (cf. 1:27), "our citizenship." Christians eagerly anticipate (*apekdechomai*) a Savior from heaven, the Lord Jesus Christ. To focus on heavenly things is the opposite of vv. 18-19 where the focus is on worldly things. Jesus is described as one "who will change (*metaschematizo*, transform) our humble bodies to the likeness (*summorphos*) of his glorious body according to his energizing power, and to subject all things to himself." The earthly body is exchanged for a glorious body (cf. 1 Cor. 15:35-51). Christ is Lord of all (Phil. 2:11; cf. 1 Cor. 15:24-28).

4:1. On the basis of these things, I urge you to stand firm in the Lord. (Additional comments on this verse are included in notes on Chapter 4.)

CHAPTER SUMMARY
Beware of false teachers who work evil and want to circumcise everybody! Christians are the new Israel, and this does not depend on human external markers. If you want to measure by the external things related to Judaism, I (Paul) come out very well: I am circumcised, genuine Israelite, tribe of Benjamin, Hebrew of the Hebrews, spotless concerning the law, Pharisee, I even persecuted the church. With regard to the righteousness of the Law, I had it made.

None of that matters to me anymore. The gain is now loss, the loss is now gain. What matters to me more than anything else is to know Christ, to be found in him, to be righteous with the righteousness of God by faith. The great goal of my life is to know Christ and the power of his resurrection, to share sufferings, to become like him in his death, and to ultimately arrive at the resurrection from the dead.

None of that is fully in place in my life, but I am trying to possess the things for which Christ possessed me. The ultimate goal is the prize for which he calls us upward. To reach the goal, I forget the past and reach forward. I hope you think the same things, and that God will make all of this clear to you so that we at least live up to God's standard considering the point to which we have progressed.

Imitate me, follow my example, because some have reverted to worldly things, appetites, shameful things, and they are enemies of Christ. With a heavenly citizenship, anticipating the Savior Jesus Christ, we think about the upward call and the ultimate resurrection and not about the things of this world. One day Jesus will change this earthly body to a glorious body like his, using his power—the same power that makes him Lord and brings everything into subjection to him.

Stand in the Lord. How much I want to see you, you are indeed my joy and crown!

Philippians 4

[Note: it is suggested that the student read the introductory materials on pages 3-8 of this guide before beginning any individual preparatory reading and analysis.]

CONTENT
The paragraphing included in the Content section of each chapter is only a suggestion or guide. The student is encouraged to identify the paragraphs and the subsections within each paragraph. The division of the biblical text into paragraphs is fairly standard in modern translations.

Outline of the Chapter
4:1-9, instructions about unity, joy, and attitudes
4:10-20, the gift received from the Philippians
4:21-23, final greetings

STUDY HELPS
4:1. Paul addresses the church affectionately. He longs (*epipotheo*) for them (cf. 1:8; 2:26) and describes them as his joy and crown (cf. 1 Thess. 2:19-20; 3:9). The word "crown" (*stephanos*) often meant a victor's crown. He tells them to stand firm (*steko*, present active imperative, persevere, stand fast). Believers stand firm, God keeps believers standing (Jude 24). The seeming paradox is easily explained when one considers multiple causation. Both are essential, neither is sufficient by itself.

4:2-9. In v. 2, it appears that two church members at Philippi were experiencing interpersonal conflict. Paul admonishes them to think (*phroneo*) the same thing in the Lord (cf. 2:1-4; note the frequent use of this verb, in the context of having the same mind, same goals, same purpose, same attitude).

4:3. Some translations treat this term of address as a name (Syzygus), but it is probably a descriptive term meaning faithful co-worker (yoke-fellow). It is a masculine noun. This person, unidentified in the text although a number of speculations have been offered, was to help (*sullambano*, hold with) the two women who had shared with Paul in the work or struggle (*sunathleo*, cf. 1:27) of the gospel. It would appear that the help would be offered in order to overcome the differences or disagreements.

The construction of the verse suggests that the additional names refer to others who have also struggled along with Paul in the cause of the gospel: Clement and the rest of the fellow workers (*sunergos*), whose names are in the book of life. Clement was a common name, likely a reference to a person otherwise unknown in the New Testament. The suggestion that this Clement is the same as Clement of Rome who wrote some 35 years later does not have any evidence to support it.

4:4-7. Rejoicing is a major theme in Philippians. Rejoicing is not the result of one's circumstances but is an attitude. Gentleness (*epieikes*, kindness, the willingness to yield) is a hallmark of the Christian. This admonition is more powerful when it is read in the context of 4:2-3. In the context of the preceding verses, the return of Jesus is a motivation for Christian living. If the phrase is understood as introducing the verses that follow, it refers to the Lord's continuing presence so that Christians know peace and are not anxious.

4:6-7. Do not be anxious (*merimnao*, give thought) for anything. Prayers (*proseuche*), supplications (*deesis*), and thanksgiving (*eucharistia*) are to be used to make your requests known to God. The peace of God that surpasses all understanding (*nous*) will guard (*phroureo*, protect) your hearts and your minds (*noema*, perceptions, thoughts) in Christ Jesus. The enemy of peace is worry. Worry is lessened when concerns are presented to God. Peace is both the absence of concern and the absence of conflict. The peace that God gives is beyond understanding, it will bring calm to the believer in a way that analyzing circumstances and seeking solutions never can. Note again Paul's phrase, "in Christ Jesus."

4:8-9. These verses emphasize the importance of what we think about. "Finally," is the same construction as in 3:1. Especially in the book of Philippians, what and how we think is supreme. The list is not long: think about things that are true (*alethes*), honorable (*semnos*), right (*dikaios*), pure (*hagnos*), lovely (*prosphiles*, acceptable), of good report (*euphemos*). If there is excellence (*arete*) and praise (*epainos*), consider (*logizomai*) these things. This verb means to reason and determine what has value and priority.

True may be contrasted with false, but also refers to a way of life. Honorable may be translated as dignified, but is translated as "grave" (august) with reference to church leaders in 1 Tim. 3:8, 11 and Tit. 2:2. Right is similar to just, meaning morally upright. Pure refers to moral purity. Lovely means likeable, bringing forth love, pleasing. Good report is literally well-spoken. The first class condition controls the last two items, assuming something as true. Excellence was a common word in Greek philosophy. Worthy of praise means approved.

4:9. Whatever you learned and received and heard and saw in me, practice (*prasso*, present active imperative) these things. The sequence is helpful: one learns mentally, one incorporates understandings into one's life by listening and watching. Christianity is not defined only by what one believes, it is also evidenced by what one does.

"The God of peace will be with you" repeats the focus on peace in v. 7.

4:10-20. The last part of the letter (only the conclusion in 4:21-23 remains) again shows the personal nature of Paul's communication with the Philippian church. He explains how he is doing and expresses his gratitude for the help and support he has received from the believers in Philippi—financial, in prayers, from Epaphroditus, and in their emotional concern.

4:10. Paul echoes the theme of joy or rejoicing: "I rejoice because you have showed your care for me again. *Anathallo* means to flourish or to flourish again." Revive is a possible translation but may leave the impression that the Philippians had been unconcerned for a time. Paul's observation is not negative. Paul's continuing explanation provides the context. You were concerned, but the time was not right (*akaireomai*, to be unseasonable, to lack opportunity). Paul uses the verb *phroneo* twice in this verse. A smooth literal reading is helpful: "I rejoiced in the Lord greatly because now again you have put forth your care (*phroneo*) for me, indeed you were concerned (*phroneo*) before but lacked opportunity." Paul is simply saying that he is aware of the reason they have not been able to assist him recently as they had in the past.

4:11-14. These verses contain no translation difficulties. Paul's purpose is to reassure the Philippians that all is going well with Paul despite his circumstances. Paul is not saying that he has not experienced problems, but that he is able to overcome even in the midst of circumstances because of his attitude. The peace of God transcends our situation. Paul is not writing about the Philippians' gifts and concern because he needs anything (I do not speak from want). I have learned to be content (*autarkes*) in whatever circumstances.

4:12. The verbs used in this verse make this an interesting sentence grammatically. Paul says, "I know...I know...I have learned." "I know" is translated from the construction, "I have seen." The idea is that one knows what one has seen or experienced firsthand.

I know how to be humbled (cf. 2:8, here the meaning is to have less than needed).

I know how to have abundance (*perisseuo*, to overflow, to have more than needed).

I have learned (*mueo*) to be satisfied (*chortazo*), to be hungry (*peinao*), to be overflowing (*perisseuo*), to have need (*hustereo*). *Mueo* can mean "to be initiated" but I prefer not to use the word "secret" in the translation. Paul's ability to know God's peace and to think like Jesus with an attitude of sacrifice and service was no secret to the Christians. If it was a secret, it was to the uninitiated and the unbelievers who could not understand the joy and sacrifice of the followers of Jesus. In this verse, Paul is expressing his trust in and dependence on God.

4:13. This verse is one of the most well-known verses in the book. "I am able to do all things through him who strengthens me." In the context, the reference is to Christ Jesus. The word Christ appears in the King James Version but is not in the oldest Greek manuscripts. "Strengthens" (present tense) suggests a continual source of strength.

4:14. Literally, "you have done well to share with me (*sugkoinoneo*) in my affliction (*thlipsis*, pressure, burdens, trouble, tribulation)." The Philippians participated with Paul in the gospel (1:5). They were concerned about Paul and they had sent him financial help.

4:15-20. Paul expands his description of the relationship he and the Philippians had shared, followed by a doxology. Paul wants the Philippians to understand that the lack of communication between them was not because of his ingratitude. It appears that some time had passed since Paul and the Philippians had been in contact (2:25-30). For this reason, Paul briefly recounts their history of sharing together.

4:15-16. The Philippian church was the only church that had shared with Paul in the initial preaching of the gospel (in giving and receiving). They were aware of this fact. They had sent multiple gifts to Paul when he was in Thessalonica (in Acts 17). This does not contradict 2 Cor. 11:8-9. First, and sufficient by itself, the plural grammatical usage would be expected even if there were only one church that had helped him. Second, Paul is not describing the same time period of his ministry.

Paul established the church at Philippi when he arrived there in Acts 16. He left under pressured circumstances, and almost immediately this new church sent him money to assist with the continuation of the mission. How different than the expectation in much mission work today! Churches are established, and instead of quickly developing the ability to assist in the spread of the gospel, they become dependent and need to receive funds, often for extended periods of time. This one factor may explain how the gospel spread so rapidly in the first century and why the contemporary church so often struggles in its efforts to spread the gospel.

4:17-18. Paul makes clear that he is not writing in the hope of receiving more help, but is rather seeking fruit that abounds (*pleonazo*) to their account (*logos*). "Account" or "credit" seems the best translation, although other options such as cause, intent, and work also make sense in the context. Paul's point is that he seeks only that they be blessed by God for the generosity they have showed toward him.

Paul has (*apecho*, I have, or I have received) all that he needs and abounds (*perisseuo*). He is fully supplied (*pleroo*) and has received what they sent by Epaphroditus. He describes their gift as a fragrant offering, acceptable sacrifice, pleasing to God.

4:19-20. Just as the Philippians have helped Paul with his needs, Paul is confident that God will supply their needs as well. This is not a promise that God will give Christians every-thing we want. Wants must be distinguished from needs. Paul had what he needed for his ministry because the Philippians had shared their abundance. When a Christian has abundance, it is a gift from God to be shared. There is no greater example of God's willingness to meet our needs than the glorious spir-itual riches he has given in Christ Jesus. The doxology of v. 20 is similar to those used by Paul in other books.

4:21-23. The final greetings of Paul to the Philippians are brief. In this section is the only use of the word "saint" in the singular in the New Testament. "Every saint" is distribu-tive and is to be applied collectively; note also the plural usage in v. 22. Those who are with Paul send greetings, especially those from the household of Caesar (cf. 1:13, likely referring to various servants, slaves, and officials).

4:23. "Spirit" is used to refer to the entire human person; the word is singular. "Your" is plural. A good paraphrase says "grace be with you all."

CHAPTER SUMMARY

I urge you to resolve conflicts and work together for the gospel.

Rejoicing is the proper Christian attitude, with gentle-ness and encouragement of others, even in times of disagree-ment. Rejoicing is possible because God takes care of our needs and gives us peace that goes beyond all that we could hope.

Let your thinking be focused on positive things, just as we have tried to give you an example. This will guarantee the presence of the God of peace in your lives.

Before I close, I want to say "thank you" again for the gifts you have sent. I rejoice that you have been able to help me again, not that you were not willing all along, but you did not have the opportunity. I do not mention this because I have any needs right now. I have experienced all kinds of things, both good and bad, and I have learned to be content in every situation. Whether satisfied or hungry, lacking or abounding, I can do everything that needs to be done through the one who strengthens me. I am grateful that you are among those who have given me strength in the gospel, especially in my times of trouble.

In fact, you were the only ones who helped me in the early days. You sent help several times when I was in Thessalonica. I do not need anything, only that you be credited with the fruit of your generosity. I have what I need, and I received what you sent by Epaphroditus. God is so good to supply everything we need. Glory to Him!

We share greetings. Greetings to everyone there; greetings from everyone here, including those from Caesar's household. Grace be with you all.

Introduction to Colossians

Colossians is unlike any other New Testament writing. While it is written by Paul and is identified as one of the Prison Epistles, the purpose of the letter is unique. It bears similarities to Ephesians, but the content of Colossians puts it in a category by itself. Colossians is a warning about the dangers of integrating competing religious or philosophical views with Christianity, because such efforts fail to honor Christ's nature and work.

Colossians was written to address false teaching that was threatening the church in Colossae. It is possible that some of the teaching had already begun to spread in other parts of Asia Minor. The problem may be summarized briefly by saying that some in the church were wanting to trying to add philosophy to Christianity. Colossians is occasional literature, written for a specific purpose at a specific time to specific people in a specific context. The applications of the book must begin with an understanding of the book in its historical context. Without an analysis of the historical and cultural context, it is impossible to understand the central message of the book. (Details of the Colossian problem, often called the Colossian heresy, are set forth in a separate section below and will be explained in more detail in the study helps and comments.)

The central theme of the book is the completeness of Jesus Christ. Jesus is presented as creator, sustainer, and redeemer (Col. 1:15-21). In the physical body of Jesus dwells divinity. Jesus is the head of the church. Jesus is Lord and therefore ruler of all creation. Colossians is the summit of New Testament Christology. Paul in Colossians shows why those who want to add something else to Christ are in error. Paul shows that those who want to integrate Christianity and philosophy have misunderstood the nature and the work of Christ. The focus is on the sufficiency of Christ.

The City

Colossae was a large commercial center. The Lycus River valley was known for its wool, especially its black wool and its purple and scarlet dyed wools. The area was characterized by volcanic activity and the city was destroyed several times throughout history, with the latest destruction being dated by Tacitus in A.D. 60 and by Eusebius in A.D. 64. The Lycus River was a tributary of the Maeander River that ran past Ephesus about 100 miles to the west on its way to the Aegean Sea. The Lycus Valley had at least three churches: Colossae, Laodicea, and Hierapolis. Since the Roman road system largely bypassed Colossae, it eventually lost its prominence. Its population was largely Gentile, but there was a significant Jewish presence as well.

Author, Date, and Recipients

Author. That Paul is the author was unanimous in early literature. Timothy was with Paul at the time of the writing and is mentioned in the salutation (see also Phil. 2:19-24, Paul was planning to send Timothy to visit the Philippians). Timothy worked with Paul in the spread of the gospel and may have served as a secretary (amanuensis). Paul is also recognized as the author of Colossians by Marcion, in the Muratorian Canon, and by various Church Fathers including Irenaeus and Clement of Alexandria in the second century.

Date. The date of this letter is linked to one of Paul's imprisonments in Ephesus, Philippi, Caesarea, or Rome. A Roman imprisonment best fits the facts of Acts. The best educated guess for the writing of Colossians is Paul's first imprisonment in Rome in the early 60s. Tychicus, along with Onesimus, probably took the letters of Colossians, Ephesians and Philemon to Asia Minor.

Here is a possible chronology of Paul's writings with locations and notations concerning their relationship to the book of Acts. Dates are approximate.

Book	Date	Place of Writing	Relationship to Acts
Galatians	50	Syrian Antioch	Acts 14:28; 15:2
1 Thessalonians	51	Corinth	Acts 18:5
2 Thessalonians	51	Corinth	
1 Corinthians	55	Ephesus	Acts 19:20
2 Corinthians	56	Macedonia	Acts 20:2
Romans	57	Corinth	Acts 20:3
Colossians	early 60s	Rome	Acts 28
Philemon	early 60s	Rome	Acts 28
Ephesians	early 60s	Rome	Acts 28
Philippians	early 60s	Rome	Acts 28
1 Timothy	63 (or later)	Macedonia	
Titus	63 ??		
2 Timothy	64-68	Rome	

Recipients. The recipients are identified as saints and faithful brothers at Colossae (1:1). Paul gives instructions that the letter be read in Laodicea (4:16, see also 2:1). The church in Colossae was likely begun by Epaphras (Col. 1:7, 8; 2:1; 4:12-13) who may have been converted to Christ during Paul's stay in Ephesus (Acts 19). It seems that the development of the churches in Asia Minor (several are mentioned in Revelation 2-3) may have occurred as a result of Paul's preaching and teaching in Ephesus, a city which served as a natural entry point to the region. Since Epaphras was with Paul in Rome (4:12), it is likely that Paul's knowledge of the problems in Colossae came through Epaphras.

Some studies suggest that the church was composed largely of Gentiles, that the letter was written primarily to Gentiles, and that the philosophical system Paul is combatting is Greek philosophy, possibly Gnosticism, or an early version of Gnosticism. Aspects of this understanding will be challenged in this study guide. While there were undoubtedly Gentiles in the church (Paul was an apostle to the Gentiles, 1:27; the recipients are described as previously alienated and hostile in mind, doing evil deeds, 1:21), there is nothing in the letter that requires a mostly Gentile church. Much in the historical-cultural context, along with aspects of the literary context, suggests the possibility of a church with a significant Jewish membership. That membership, as well as the Jewish community in Colossae, was significantly Hellenized based on the context and the content of the letter.

The text of Col. 2:11-15 (where the recipients are described as dead in trespasses and fleshly uncircumcision, 2:13) is often understood as a reference to Jewish circumcision. When these verses are read in context, these verses are not a reference to Jewish circumcision. The circumcision being described is the "circumcision of Christ." This point is explained in more detail in the study notes on the paragraph.

The Colossian Heresy

Summary. The problem at Colossae was apparently the result of some teachers who wanted to integrate another religious or philosophical system with Christianity. They did not reject Christianity, but they were teaching that various add-ons or supplements were necessary to be a good Christian. Based on Colossians 2, their teaching seems to be a combination of Christianity, philosophy, and certain requirements from Judaism.

Aspects of the heresy that Paul combats. Paul specifically attacks the heresy in Col. 2:8-23. Based on the content of Paul's assertions, we can identify the following problems with the teaching: denial that the fullness of the Godhead (Deity) could dwell bodily in Christ (2:9), denial that it was possible to be complete in Christ (2:10), suggestion that genuine Christian spirituality required additional supplements or add-ons. The higher level of spirituality involved other principalities and powers (2:15), various practices that appear to be rooted in Judaism (2:16-17), self-abasement or self-degradation (2:18), the worship of angels (2:18), and various aspects of asceticism (2:19-23). (See comments on Col. 2:8-23 for a fuller description of the significance of Paul's teachings and how Paul's declarations correspond to the false philosophical system.)

Based on references throughout the letter, the false teachers can be described with the following seven points.

- They offered a "fullness" spiritually that had not been experienced before, a new type of spirituality or a new way to bring believers to maturity. The original reception of the gospel had left the new converts as second-class citizens, and thus they needed this additional experience of "fullness."
- They spoke of a new spiritual "liberty." Paul describes this as a new form of slavery.

- They alleged a personal vision of the invisible evil powers, bringing special privileges to a select group of the spiritual elite.
- They practiced an impressive asceticism, but it had not been shown to be effective in the battle against self-indulgence.
- They offered initiation to a more profound "knowledge" of God and a greater experience of God's power.
- They saw themselves as superior to, and were thus critical of, "ordinary" believers.
- They caused division in the church by their teachings and influence, a problem Paul combats with a focus on Christian unity.

Failure to understand Christ. When some are wanting to add to the message and work of Christ, the problem is a failure to understand the person and work of Christ. To combat the false theological and philosophical teaching, Paul emphasizes the uniqueness of Christ's person, the deity of Christ, the all-sufficient saving work of Christ, and the Lordship of Jesus. Paul shows the inadequacy of the alternative understanding. He describes it as hollow and deceptive (2:8) and notes that it is unable to restrain physical desires. Believers have fullness in Christ (2:10) so that nothing added can contribute to the salvation that Christ gives.

Is the philosophy in question Judaism? In the first century, Judaism was often referred to as a philosophy. The Jewish philosopher Philo (born c. 20 B.C., died A.D. 40-50, the exact dates are in question) described the Torah as the "philosophy of Moses." He referred to Judaism as "the philosophy of our fathers." Josephus wrote about three Jewish sects describing them as "three philosophies." It seems this was done to add dignity to Judaism. (See below for more about how Philo helped shape Jewish thought in the first century, especially with reference to the desire to integrate Judaism and Greek philosophy.)

Against this background, Paul's description (2:8) of the empty and deceptive philosophy takes on new possibilities. Paul is not objecting to philosophical thinking. He is objecting to the particular philosophy known to his readers, a philosophy that he calls a vain deceit. The most likely meaning of this phrase is this: "Let no one take advantage of you through the empty deceit of Jewish philosophy." That Paul uses the article, "the philosophy," is interesting for it indicates a specific thought system and not a generalized criticism of philosophy.

The heresy was about the need for spiritual supplements. The heretics were not denying the value of Christianity, they were saying that more was needed for salvation. (Think about the Galatian Judaizers who insisted on adding circumcision as a requirement to be genuinely Christian.) They were looking for spiritual supplements, ceremonial laws, an attitude of humility or self-abnegation, angel worship, and a form of asceticism. They were puffed up, no longer connected with the head. These false teachers were Christians, not outsiders. They held Christ, they had not rejected him; they were believers not unbelievers, but they wanted to place additional requirements on Christianity. They taught that additional requirements were necessary to reach authentic spirituality. Paul's references to circumcision are often read to suggest that the teachers were Jewish, but there is no specific reference to Jewish circumcision in the text (see study helps and comments on 2:11-14).

The Influence of Philo in First-Century Judaism

That the false teachers at Colossae were likely Jews is supported by an understanding of how Judaism was developing in the time of Christ and shortly after. A major factor in this process was the influence of Philo, a Jewish philosopher from Alexandria. Philo spans the Greek and Hebrew cultures. When Hebrew thought with its focus on the invisible, mystical, and unknown, met Greek philosophical thought, it was natural to try to develop philosophical justification for, or at least explanations of, Judaism. Philo provided a synthesis of the two thought systems and influenced Hellenistic interpretation of Messianic Hebrew thought for the next two to three centuries.

For Philo, Greek philosophy was the natural development of the revelation given by God to Moses. He was not the first to try to describe the relationship between the Old Testament and Greek philosophy. Jewish scholars before him had made the same effort, especially in the two centuries before Jesus after the translation of the Septuagint (LXX), a translation of the Hebrew Old Testament into Greek. There was even a tradition that said the books of Moses were translated into Greek long before the LXX.

Purpose of the Letter

Theme. The theme of Colossians is Jesus Christ. Paul wants to show that Christ is adequate and that no religious or philosophical system can add anything of value to the work of Christ. A clear understanding of Christ is the antidote to false teaching that seeks supplements to the message of Christ. Paul's first line of defense against the heresy was to exalt Christ. Christ is the very image of God (1:15), the Creator (1:16), the sustainer of all things (1:17), the head of the church (1:18), the firstborn from the dead (1:18), preeminent (1:18), the fullness of deity in bodily form (1:19, 2:9), the reconciler between God and mankind (1:20-22). Christ is completely adequate for salvation. The word Christ is used 25 times in 95 verses.

Background. In this study, the purpose of the letter is seen through the following lens.

The church at Colossae was composed of both Jews and Gentiles. Paul had never visited that church, but as apostle to the Gentiles, Paul was concerned when teaching was introduced at Colossae that sought to add certain elements to faith in Christ, thus denying the sufficiency of Christ and the fullness possible in Christ. These additional items Paul describes as a philosophical system that is empty and deceitful.

In the first century, some Jews were seeking to integrate Judaism and Greek philosophy. The result was an understanding that described Judaism as a philosophy. Some at Colossae were thinking that if such an effort worked to better explain Judaism, it would also work for Christianity. The result was a complex conglomeration of Christian ideas, Roman philosophy (possibly including incipient Gnosticism), and Judaism.

To combat this effort, Paul sets forth the sufficiency of Christ, citing also his own calling to proclaim Christ. The heretical teachings would serve to enslave Christians in human traditions, human teachings, and worldly values. All such things were cast off by "the circumcision of Christ," which has nothing to do with the circumcision made with hands (Jewish circumcision) but has to do with putting off fleshly concerns for spiritual concerns.

The "circumcision of Christ" occurred at baptism, so that afterward God's power made it possible to be raised with Christ. The result was that those who were dead in sin (before the old man was cut away and cast off) were made alive with Christ and forgiven. The IOUs and legal demands that we had as a result of sin were cancelled. These were set aside by Christ's death on the cross, when he took away the power of all other authorities and rulers. He took away their reputation (shamed them) when he completely triumphed over them.

Do not let anyone judge you or exclude you on the basis of such requirements. You escaped such things when you died with Christ. Because you are risen with Christ, you can focus on things above and not on worldly things. Therefore, follow through on the "circumcision of Christ" by putting off the old self and putting on the new self. Christ is everything!

Let your life reflect the new self in attitudes, actions, relationships, and how you tell others about Christ.

Purpose. Paul wants to make clear why the false teaching that is being advanced is erroneous. To do this, Paul exalts Christ to demonstrate that the philosophy being advanced by the false teachers is in error. Paul describes Christ's saving work that separated us from worldly concerns in our baptism and raised us with him to a new life. Paul describes the lifestyle of the new self because living a new life is what Christianity is all about.

The Literary Relationship between Ephesians and Colossians

The literary relationship between Ephesians and Colossians is best understood against the backdrop of the historical relationship between Colossians and Ephesians.

Colossians. Epaphras (Col. 1:7; 4:12; Philemon 23) was apparently converted during Paul's Ephesian ministry (Acts 19). It is likely that he was instrumental in starting three churches-- in Hierapolis, Laodicea and Colossae. When difficulties arose in the Colossian church (relating to the emerging desire to integrate worldviews and religious systems), Epaphras sought the advice of Paul who was at that time in prison in Rome (in the early 60s).

When Paul received information about the problem in Colossae, a church which he had never personally visited, he wrote a letter focused on the lordship and sufficiency of Jesus. The letter is brief and is characterized by short sentences.

Ephesians. At about the same time, Paul wrote a more thoughtful treatise on the same theme—the lordship of Jesus and the importance of this concept for a proper understanding of God's saving work in Christ according to his eternal purpose in Christ, to bring everything together under the headship of Jesus in the church which is the body of Christ, which is the basis for the unity of the church. This letter is known as Ephesians, and may have been a circular letter intended to be distributed to several churches. Ephesians is characterized by long sentences and theological development.

Relationship. Factors that are often cited in demonstrating a close relationship between Ephesians and Colossians include (1) related literary and theological themes and structure, dealing with the same general topics, (2) similar salutations and similar closings, (3) similar words and phrases (as many as 75 of the verses in Ephesians have a parallel in Colossians), (4) Paul's authorship, and (5) both were delivered by Tychicus.

These similarities may lead one to overlook the differences in the letters. Both are occasional literature, written to a specific location at a specific time, to specific people to address a specific situation. Ephesians focuses on God's eternal purpose, accomplished in the saving work of Jesus, resulting in the unified church that brings together all the saved regardless of ethnicity. Colossians focuses on Christ as divine, Creator, Sustainer, Savior, but the point is to show the adequacy of Christ and to demonstrate that any supplements are not only unnecessary but that they deny the spiritual reality of Christ. In Colossians one encounters teachings designed to combat dualism. Colossians focuses on the problem of syncretism—the integration of religious systems.

In summary, both Ephesians and Colossians are among Paul's four prison letters. Some of the themes of the books are similar, with similar wording and phrases. Colossians was written to combat specific Christological misunderstandings and to speak against false teachers who were trying to integrate Christianity and Jewish philosophy. Ephesians was written to encourage the Ephesian church (and perhaps other churches, if it is understood as a circular letter) toward unity and Christian living on the basis of God's eternal purpose in Christ and the church.

General Outline of the Letter to the Colossians

The book seems to divide naturally into two parts (as do many of Paul's letters). These are variously described as teaching and application, pedagogy and practice, explanation and exhortation. The common division is set forth here. (See the comments beginning at 2:20 for alternative outlining and divisions.)

Chapters 1-2, the sufficiency of Jesus

Chapters 3-4, how to live a life consistent with the new life in Jesus, who is all in all

A more detailed outline includes these major units.

1:1-14, traditional salutation, thanksgiving and prayer, theme statement about Christ

1:15-23, the nature and work of Christ

1:24-2:5, Paul's ministry for the cause of Christ

2:6-19, warnings and admonitions about the philosophy advanced by the false teachers

2:20-23, "having died with Christ" empowers Christian living

3:1-4, "having been raised with Christ" empowers Christian living

3:5-11, putting off worldly things

3:12-17, putting on Christ

3:18-4:1, relationships in Christ

4:2-6, instructions

4:9-18, final greetings

Gnosticism

While the influence of Gnosticism is most visible in the late first century and in the second century after Christ, some have identified evidences of the influence of an incipient Gnosticism as early as the 60s. Because it is possible that efforts to integrate Jewish thought and Greek philosophy were influenced by early forms of Gnosticism, a brief overview is included here.

Before 1945 Gnosticism was known only from counter arguments, but the Nag Hammadi texts, discovered in 1945 in a jar full of Gnostic books, have given new insights. Based on the Dead Sea Scrolls, discovered in 1947, it appears that the Essenes also cultivated some Gnostic ideas.

The Gnostics were dualists, seeing matter and spirit as antagonistic, and for this reason denied that Jesus could be both fully man and fully divine. Their conclusion was that Jesus was divine but not human. The Gnostics identified angelic levels (*aeons*) as steps between humanity and the good high god. Jesus could be no more than one of the gods. The Gnostics tended to be intellectually elite and emphasized secret knowledge as the path to the gods (or for Christians who accepted Gnostic thought, to God). This secret knowledge was the true key to fellowship with God rather than Jesus' atoning work to make possible forgiveness.

The problem at Colossae was that some teachers were advancing a hybrid version of Christianity. The false teachers were not absolutely rejecting Christ, and it is not clear that the specific false philosophy addressed in Colossians was Gnosticism. What can be said is that Paul was combatting teachings that sought to integrate Christianity and philosophy, and that the philosophy Paul addressed bore marks of influences from Greek thought, Judaism, and possibly an early form of Gnosticism.

After the more complete development of the concepts, second century Gnosticism reveals the following beliefs:

- Matter and spirit are co-eternal. Matter is evil, spirit is good. God who is spirit and therefore good cannot be involved with evil.
- There are levels (*aeons*, emanations) between matter and divinity. The lowest level of divinity is YHWH of the Old Testament because he formed matter as he formed the world.
- Jesus is higher than YHWH on the levels, closer to the true divine nature. Some Christians influenced by Gnosticism put Jesus at the highest level but could not accept that he was incarnate Deity. Remember: matter is evil; therefore Jesus could not have a human body and still be

divine. The solution to the problem was the theory that Jesus only appeared to be human.

- Salvation is defined as passing through the various heavenly spheres, and comes through faith in Jesus plus special knowledge that is available only to a limited group.

- The Gnostics arrived at two opposite ethical systems. One said that lifestyle had nothing to do with salvation, and that salvation was available by the secret knowledge that allowed one to pass through the angelic spheres. The other said that lifestyle was essential. In Colossians, on the basis of the ascetic teachings (2:16-23), it appears that the false teachers were focused on lifestyle as an evidence of true spirituality.

Colossians 1

[Note: it is suggested that the student read the introductory materials on pages 3-8 of this guide before beginning an individual preparatory reading and analysis.]

CONTENT

The paragraphing included in the Content section of each chapter provides suggestions or guides for your own work. The student is encouraged to identify the paragraphs, and sub-sections within each paragraph, to assist in personal study. The division of the biblical text into paragraphs is fairly standard in recent translations.

Outline of the Chapter

1:1-2, salutation and greetings

1:3-8, thanksgiving and prayer

1:9-14, the saving work of Christ

> *Note: vv. 13-14 are transitional, paragraphing could be 9-13, 14-23.*

1:15-23, the preeminence and supremacy of Christ's reconciling work

[1:21-23, the result of Christ's work in the lives of the Colossians]

> *Note: vv. 9-20 are one extended sentence in Greek, so*
> *vv. 21-23 may be better understood as a separate section.*

1:24-2:5, the sacrificial ministry of Paul, apostle to the Gentiles, his focus on God's plan

STUDY HELPS

1:1-2. As he introduces a book designed to combat false teaching, Paul identifies himself as an apostle. This word is used at times in the New Testament in a non-technical way to describe those sent as representatives of another person or of the churches. Here Paul uses the term in an official way as evidence of the authority of his teaching. Paul strengthens his self-description as an apostle by adding "of Christ Jesus" (that is, he was sent by Christ, having personally encountered him on the Damascus road), and "by the will of God." The latter phrase he uses also in the salutations of 1 Corinthians, 2 Corinthians, Ephesians, and 2 Timothy.

Timothy, Paul's co-laborer in the gospel, is identified as "our brother." Timothy is also included in the greetings of 2 Corinthians, Philippians, 1 Thessalonians, 2 Thessalonians, and Philemon. This indicates Timothy's presence with Paul. It does not mean that Timothy is a co-author of the book.

The recipients are identified as saints (holy ones) and faithful brothers in Christ at Colossae. In a letter that will focus on correcting false teaching, it may be significant that Paul says he is writing to the faithful Christians in the church. "In Christ" is sometimes used in parallel to "in the church" since the church is the body of Christ (1:18). Grace and peace are characteristic of Paul's greetings. The textual variant that would add "and our Lord Jesus Christ" to the phrase "from God our Father" does not change the interpretation of the text.

1:3-8. Some outlines suggest that Colossians opens with two prayers of Paul (1:3-8 and 1:9-14), others think it better to understand the opening as one prayer with two parts. In this study, the prayer of Paul will be analyzed as two separate paragraphs. The first part of the passage (vv. 3-8) is one sentence in Greek, representing one continuous prayer or thought.

Paul often mentions his prayers and thanksgiving for the churches in the salutations of his letters. As we read this salutation (and others in Paul's writings), it is easy to forget that Paul was writing under difficult circumstances. Paul is constantly (always) praying and giving thanks for the Colossians. Paul is grateful for their faith and love. That he has only heard of their faith may reflect the fact that Paul had apparently never been to Colossae. Paul was receiving this news from Epaphras (v. 7) from whom they had learned the gospel.

Paul frequently uses "faith, hope, and love" together (vv. 4-5). Paul has already described the recipients as faithful (v. 2). Here their faith in Christ (*en*, in contrast to the more common Pauline proposition *eis*) may refer to their faithfulness, or it may focus on the fact that at a time in the past they had recognized the truth of the gospel message about Jesus and had responded in faith. The second meaning would be especially important in view of the subject of the letter. They have put their faith "in Christ" (*en* is locative), not "in Christ plus various supplements."

Another basis for Paul's gratitude was their love for one another, or their love for the brotherhood of Christians. "All the saints" could have either meaning in the context, foreshadowing Paul's correction of the false teachers who were apparently drawing lines of fellowship that excluded some Christians or identified them as less than faithful.

1:5-6. The faith and love of the Colossians was "because of (*dia*) the hope laid up for them in heaven." Hope is something Christians have in the present tense; hope is also described as something that awaits the Christian, that is, hope that is reserved and will one day be fully realized. This goal is described as glory, salvation, eternal life, and inheritance in other New Testament texts. The Christian hope is the result of God's work (laid up for you) and cannot be altered by human declarations to the contrary, again anticipating the heresy Paul will address in this letter. The Colossians had heard about this hope through the truth of the gospel. The gospel is truth; when the gospel is proclaimed, truth is heard. The gospel had sounded forth and was bearing fruit and growing. "In all the world" in this context is hyperbole (overstatement), referring to the then-known Greco-Roman world. The gospel was to be preached everywhere (see the use of the same phrase in the Great Commission, Matt. 28:19-20; Luke 24;46-47; cf. Acts 1:8).

The Colossians had understood (*eipgnosko*, to fully know, to have intimate knowledge) the grace of God in truth (v. 6, the gospel). The intensified form of *gnosko* may anticipate the heretical emphasis on special knowledge (cf. 1:9, 10).

1:7-8. The role of Epaphras in the establishment of the church in Colossae (cf. Col. 4:12-13; Philm. 23) has already been explained in the introduction. Here Epaphras is identified as a faithful (note the repeated emphasis on faith and faithfulness) servant of Christ. He had reported to Paul and those with Paul the love "in spirit" of the Colossians. This is traditionally translated as a reference to the Holy Spirit (which would be the only reference to the Holy Spirit in the book), but it is also possible to understand a reference to the human spirit, thus "heart-felt love."

1:9-20. As mentioned in the outline above, the paragraphing is difficult. Verses 9-20 are one extended sentence in Greek, with each thought building on the previous ones, thus making it difficult to establish the thematic sub-sections. In vv. 9-12, Paul describes his prayer for the continued future growth of the church. In v. 13-14 he summarizes the Father's redemptive work through the Son. He uses that summary as a springboard for vv. 15-20 which may be a hymn or poem describing the supremacy of Christ. Verse 20 ends the long sentence. Then vv. 21-23 are parallel to and an expansion of vv. 13-14, again describing the result of Christ's nature and work in the Colossian church (so that vv. 13-14 and vv. 21-23 serve as parentheses around the poetic section).

Some see the poetic section as including only vv. 15-18 since v. 19 begins with "for" (*oti*). The continuation of the extended sentence makes it better to understand that the poetic section is vv. 15-20 (as reflected in the NET Bible). This section is one of the great Christological confessions of the New Testament.

1:9-14. Because of the things included in vv. 3-8, especially the faith and love of the Colossians that had been reported to Paul, Paul mentions in v. 9 the "without ceasing" prayer for the Colossians (either Paul using an editorial "we" or referring to himself and those with him). Paul is praying that the Colossians "be filled...to walk...."

To identify paragraphs and outline a section, often the first step is to diagram the sentences. In diagraming sentences, the first step is to identify the subject and the verb. This provides the skeleton of the sentence on which the other details depend. (The English translations we have access to often make this difficult.) "So that you will be filled..." (aorist passive subjunctive) is the main verb of vv. 9-12. The construction of the verbs related to the Colossians is this: "so you will <u>be filled</u>, to <u>walk</u>, <u>bearing fruit</u>, <u>growing</u>, <u>being strengthened</u>, <u>giving thanks</u> to the Father." The main verb is followed by an infinitive (to walk) and four dependent participles that show the method or results of being filled to walk. The "you" refers to the Colossians.

In vv. 12-13, the construction of the verbs related to the Father is this: the Father [is] the one <u>enabling</u> us, who <u>rescued</u> us, and <u>transferred</u> us.

In v. 14, Paul writes that "we have" redemption and forgiveness, including himself with the Colossians, extending to all Christians.

1:9. Paul prays and asks that the Colossians will be filled (*pleroo*) with knowledge (*epignosis*, the intensified form may mean full knowledge or intimate knowledge) in wisdom (*sophia*, see also 1:28; 2:3, 23; 3:16; 4:5) and understanding (*sunesis*, see 2:2) in order to walk (a metaphor that means to live) in a certain way. Notice the connection between what we know and how we live. It is impossible to live according to God's will if we do not know God's will, and the knowledge of God's will requires wisdom and discernment. This verse foreshadows the focus of the false teachers. They sought secret knowledge (2:3).

1:10-12. The Christian walk is described as worthy (*axios*) and pleasing, with four participial phrases following.

"Bearing fruit in every good work" (*karpophoreo*, this verb combines the words for fruit and to bring forth). The Christian lives in such a way that she or he bears fruit.

"Growing in knowledge" (*epignosko,* see 3:10) is a present participle indicating that this is a continuous process.

"Being strengthened with power" uses the same root word twice (*dunamis, dunamoo,* power or strength); literally, the meaning is "with all strength being strengthened." "According to his glorious might" uses a synonym for power (*kratos,* might). The Christian life is lived by God's power that enables the believer. "With joy" can be understood as the last part of the phrase in v. 11, or it may introduce v. 12: joyfully giving thanks.

"Giving thanks" is the last of the four participles (see 3:17).

1:12-13. The Father is described with a participial phrase that functions as an adjective: "the Father, the one enabling (*hikanoo*, the root signifies being sufficient) us to share the inheritance." Light contrasts with the use of darkness in the next phrase. The Father has done two things: he rescued us (*rhuomai*, to deliver) from the dominion (*exousia*, authority) of darkness and transferred (literally, to put in a new place, relocate) us to the kingdom of "the son of his love" (or "his beloved son," referring to Jesus).

1:14. In Jesus, "we have redemption, the forgiveness of sins."

1:15-20. This poetic section, possibly a hymn or creedal statement, summarizes the sufficiency and supremacy of Christ as sovereign—reigning, redeeming, and reconciling. Catching the attention of the careful reader is the repeated use of the word "all" in this section. Another repeated construction is built around the prepositions preceding "him"—in him, through him, for him.

Exalting Jesus
Jesus is....
The revealing one
The reigning one
The redeeming one
The reconciling one

1:15. "...who is image (*eikon*) of the invisible God..." Jesus in his humanity makes the invisible visible (John 14:9). Jesus in his humanity, bearing the image of God, declares possible the restoration of the relationship broken by the entry of sin to the world (see Gen. 1:26-27; 3:1-5).

"firstborn of all creation..." This word can refer to time (first in order chronologically) or to rank. To be firstborn meant to have preeminence. The firstborn had privilege, possessions, and received the birthright. In Ps. 89:27, firstborn has a Messianic sense as it describes the anointed chosen king. Here the word refers to Jesus' rank over creation. The phrase does not declare that Jesus was created or born, or that there was a time when Jesus did not exist. Jesus was uniquely the Son of God, always existing, always Deity, even before creation (1:16-17). This description of Jesus is a declaration of preeminence over (before) all creation.

1:16. "for all things were created by him..." Jesus was the agent of the creation of "all things." Included are things in the heavenly and earthly realms, things visible and invisible, and all power structures—thrones, dominions, principalities, and powers. Because Jesus is creator of all, he is before all and above all. Creation was in (*en*) him, by (*dia*) him, and for (*eis*) him. The idea of God's involvement in the creation of the material world speaks against dualism, the philosophical view that separates spirit (God) and matter.

1:17. "He himself is before all things and in him all things are set together." In this context, to be before all things refers to his preexistence as Deity. The noun is intensified (he himself), both here and in v. 18. In him all things consist (perfect active indicative from *sunistao*, or *sunistemi,* to be set together, to stand together). The action has been completed. All things have been set together in creation and Jesus is sustainer as well as creator.

1:18. "He himself is head of the body the church..." The metaphor makes clear the relationship between Christ and the church. He is head of the body. Jesus is described as "head" of the church only in Ephesians and Colossians, although the church is also described as the body in 1 Cor. 12.

"...who is the beginning, the firstborn from the dead, in order that he himself may become in everything 'being first.'" Beginning is *arche*, the same word that was translated principalities in v. 16. This is most likely a reference to origin or source, with the primary reference being to the church. Firstborn (*prototokos*) is the same word as in v. 15. It is best understood as having the same meaning in both verses (v. 15 and v. 18). The reference is to Jesus' preeminence, not to his resurrection from the dead. Remember that there were resurrections during Jesus' ministry prior to Jesus' resurrection. The reference to rank rather than chronology is reinforced in the last part of the verse. All of this points to Jesus as "being first" (*proteuo*) and having supremacy or preeminence.

1:19. Because (*oti*) this is God's will... That is, it pleased God for all the fullness to dwell in Christ. The purpose clause that introduces this verse also introduces v. 20. The fullness refers to the fullness of Deity (see 2:9). Jesus was fully divine. The use of the word fullness (*pleroma*) may foreshadow some of the false teaching in which "fullness" was used in a different sense.

1:20. "And to reconcile all things through him..." God's purpose in Christ was to reconcile (*apokatallasso*, to reconcile fully) all things to himself through (*dia*) Christ. In the context, the phrase "all things" has previously been used to refer to all creation. We see repetition also in the phrase "whether things on earth or things in heaven." Reconciliation is "to make friends again." The relationship between God and human creation was broken by sin. With the entry of sin into the world, humanity became the enemy of God (Rom. 5:10). The result of reconciliation is the restoration of fellowship resulting in peace. Peace is possible because of the blood shed on the cross. Jesus shed human blood to reconcile us to God. It is possible that the false teachers were denying Jesus' humanity, affirming only his deity. Here ends the extended sentence in vv. 9-20.

1:21-23. In these verses is a brief description of the results of Christ's work in the lives of the Colossians. Some authors suggest that the "you" of v. 21 and the accompanying description can apply only to Gentiles, that such words cannot be used to describe the Jews. However, since the alienation and hostility are mental processes and provide a description of a separation to be mended with reconciliation in Christ, one can understand without much difficulty the possibility of such descriptions applied to both Gentiles and Jews. Certainly, the Jews were accused of evil deeds in the Old Testament, and during his ministry Jesus said that people rejected the light because of their evil deeds (John 3:19-20). In the context of John 3, this has a primary application to Jews. In v. 21, the condition of the mind is demonstrated by actions. The strongest evidence of the application of v. 21 to both Jews and Gentiles is that vv. 22-23 most certainly apply to all of the Christians at Colossae, whether Jew or Gentile.

One aspect of the Colossian heresy that Paul will address in detail in Chapter 2 involves the desire of some to require certain Jewish practices as evidence of success in Christian living (see my Introduction to Colossians). In various references in the first chapter, we can see that Paul is preparing for his argument. Every Christian, regardless of ethnicity, has been reconciled to God, thereby escaping alienation and enmity. This reconciliation God accomplished by making peace through Jesus' blood shed on the cross (v. 20).

1:22. The reconciliation God accomplished in Jesus is the primary topic of vv. 20-23. God has acted to redeem all humanity. God has reconciled "in the physical body through death" to present (aorist active infinitive) "you" holy, without blemish, and without blame. The past tense infinitive most likely refers to their salvation by Christ's death, but can be applied also to their continuing state in Christ, showing that additional things are not needed to bring the believer to holiness and blamelessness.

1:23. The results of God's reconciliation are not unconditional. To the reconciliation from God that presented the Colossian believers as holy in God's presence is now added a condition. "If you continue..." This is a first class condition which is assumed to be true. The Colossians will continue to stand before God holy, without blemish, and blameless if they persevere in faith (faithfulness) to Christ. Continuing requires belief, action, and relationship. Paul describes the life of the believer in Christ—established (*themelioo*, to lay a foundation, to ground) and steadfast (*hedraios*, immovable) and not moved (*metakineo*, to remove) from the hope of the gospel. The gospel had been proclaimed to all creation, referring to the then-known world, or perhaps to the Roman Empire (see my comments on 1:6). Paul is himself a servant (*diakonos*) of this gospel.

1:24-29. (The paragraph continues through 2:5, but the comments on the paragraph will break at the chapter division and be continued under 2:1-5.)

1:24. "I rejoice in sufferings for you..." Paul saw that his suffering, perhaps a reference to his imprisonment although Paul had suffered many things for the gospel (2 Cor. 11:23-28), was on behalf of those who would hear the gospel. Paul's view of suffering is not a popular message in churches today. Most do not understand rejoicing in suffering, and few are willing to suffer for others.

Paul's next statement is difficult to grasp. "I fill up the things lacking of the afflictions of Christ in my flesh on behalf of his body which is the church." An adjustment of word order helps a little. "In my physical body I fill up (I complete), for the sake of his body the church, what is lacking in Christ's sufferings." Although some have theorized that Christ's atonement was insufficient, from which Roman Catholicism developed a system of human merit, this is not true biblically, and would certainly not fit into the context of Colossians where Paul is attempting to show the total sufficiency of Christ's person and work. Paul recognized his suffering as necessary to complete God's work in Christ. Christ suffered for us and did all that was necessary for our reconciliation. We can also expect to suffer on behalf of the gospel and the building up of the church.

1:25. Paul was a servant (*diakonos*) of the church and a servant of the gospel (v. 23), through his proclamation of God's word. He had received a commission (*oikonomia*, usually translated stewardship, referring to a task or obligation) from God. This commission called him to complete (*pleroo*, fully complete, perhaps in the sense of "to fully carry out") the task of preaching the word of God.

1:26. Paul describes the message to be preached as the mystery now made manifest. In Scripture, "mystery" signifies something previously unknown but now revealed (see Eph. 3:3). With this declaration, Paul describes himself as recipient of God's revelation, anticipating those false teachers who would claim access to special revelation and knowledge. The mystery has been made manifest to the saints (all Christians), denying the claim of the false teachers to have special knowledge of God's mystery. What was formerly hidden has now been made known.

1:27. God wanted to make known to the saints the glorious riches of the mystery among the Gentiles. The mystery, as Paul describes it in Eph. 3:2-6, is the inclusion of both Jews and Gentiles together in the church. God's eternal plan was to unite Jews and Gentiles together as heirs, participants and sharers in Christ, that is, in the church. God's eternal goal, formerly not revealed, was to provide glorious riches to all humanity: "Christ in you, the hope of glory." This is usually interpreted as Christ's indwelling (cf. Eph. 3:17), but grammatically it could also be translated "Christ among you," signifying the mystery of the gospel as it came to both Jewish believers and Gentile believers in Colossae. The verse has two parallel constructions: the mystery among (*en*) the Gentiles; Christ in (*en*) you. To be dogmatic in ambiguous matters seldom serves us well, but in the context, these seem parallel and "among" is perhaps the stronger translation option: Christ among you Jewish and Gentile believers is the source of hope (again showing that nothing else is needed).

1:28-29. Paul's goal is to proclaim Christ. His focus is on Christ. As Paul proclaims Christ, he does two things with one purpose in mind. He admonishes and he teaches to present every person complete in Christ. Admonish (*noutheteo*) is used of training children and of encouraging one another. "Every man" uses the word (*anthropos*) that refers to human beings irrespective of gender. The phrase is repeated for emphasis three times. Paul seeks to include all; the false teachers were trying to exclude and made it difficult to enter the "inner circle." Teaching (*didasko*) is to be done with all wisdom (anticipating the 'false' wisdom of the heretical teachers). Paul's goal is to present every person complete (*teleios*, mature) in Christ. Every Christian can reach maturity. In Christ, there is no place for special privilege and elitism.

This work that God has given Paul calls for labor (*kopiao*) and struggle (*agonizomai*). Notice the root of our word agony. God's work is not easy, but it is done with the power (*energeia*) of God that is at work (*energeo*) within his people, literally the energy that energizes us.

CHAPTER SUMMARY

Paul writes to faithful members of the church at Colossae, with thanksgiving and prayer, noting how their faith and love in Christ have developed since they heard and accepted the gospel message of hope. The gospel has grown and borne fruit everywhere it has gone in all the world, and it has done the same among the Colossians, according to the report of Epaphras who had proclaimed the gospel in Colossae.

Paul prays for their knowledge, wisdom, and insight of God's will so they will live lives that are worthy and pleasing. The evidence of such lives is seen in the fruit of good works, growth in knowledge, spiritual strength, and joyful gratitude to God. God is the one who has enabled their inheritance in the light; he has rescued them from darkness and has transferred them to the kingdom of his beloved Son where they have redemption.

Considering what is known of Jesus Christ, this work of God that God has accomplished through his Son is significant and complete! Jesus is the image of God making visible the things that are invisible. He is the firstborn preeminent one over all creation. In fact, all things were created by him, including whatever powers exist. Jesus existed first and he now holds everything together. He is head of the church, as well as the source or beginning, preeminent in all things. It pleased the Father for all divine fullness to dwell in the Son, to reconcile all things through the Son, to make peace. Jesus is supreme.

The work of God changes everything. Before they heard the gospel, they used to think like strangers and enemies of God, and they lived the same way. Now God has reconciled them through Jesus' physical death, and they are no longer strangers and enemies—they are reconciled to stand before him holy, unblemished, and blameless. This change will continue to characterize their lives if they remain faithful, grounded firmly in the hope they have found in the gospel. Paul is a servant of this gospel as it is preached in all the world.

Paul rejoices in all his sufferings that have helped bring the gospel to them. Christ's sufferings are being fulfilled in his sufferings. The church is established only through sufferings—first Christ's, then ours. God commissioned Paul as a servant with them in mind, to proclaim God's word that was formerly unknown. Now the mystery has been revealed to Christians. This mystery brings glorious riches among the Gentiles. This mystery is Christ among you, Christ among us. This is the glorious message of hope.

All of this Paul wants to communicate when he preaches Christ. By preaching, instructing, and teaching everyone, Paul is trying to present everyone complete in Christ. He is working and struggling toward this goal, but the real power is the energy with which God energizes him.

Colossians 2

[Note: it is suggested that the student read the introductory materials on pages 3-8 of this guide before beginning an individual preparatory reading and analysis.]

CONTENT

The paragraphing examples included in the Content section of each chapter are merely suggestions or guides. The student is encouraged to identify the paragraphs, and subsections within each paragraph, to assist in his or her own study. The division of the biblical text into paragraphs is fairly consistent in modern translations.

Outline of the Chapter

2:1-5, Paul's ministry and his concern for the Colossians described (1:24-2:5)

2:6-19, not philosophy, but Christ alone; warnings against false teaching

2:20-3:4, new life in Christ
> *Note: the larger paragraph likely encompasses 2:20-3:17.*

STUDY HELPS

2:1-5. These verses are the conclusion of the paragraph that began in 1:24. Notes and comments on that paragraph are continued here, honoring the traditional chapter division.

  2:1-2. Paul's struggle (*agon*, conflict, fight, race) was spiritual, perhaps in prayer or emotional stress. Some translators refer to his "hard work" for those in Colossae and Laodicea, even though he had never been there. Others take this as a reference to his ministry to the Gentiles, assuming a largely Gentile church. The reason for Paul's struggle is described with a subordinate clause, reflected in this literal translation: "in order that their hearts may be comforted (aorist passive subjunctive, *parakaleo*), having been united (*sumbibazo*) in (*en*) love, and unto (*eis*) all the richness (cf. 1:27) of the full assurance (*plerophoria*) of the understanding (*sunesis*), unto (*eis*) full knowledge (*epignosis*) of the mystery of God—Christ..." The participle form "being united" controls the three phrases that follow it: being united—in love, unto all richness of confidence of knowledge, unto full knowledge... Analyzing the relationship between the nouns show that the focus of Paul's conflict for the Colossians is "that their hearts may be comforted, having been united in love, resulting in the riches that come from full confidence of understanding, resulting in true knowledge of God's mystery, which is Christ." Christ is the means of the mystery. In Ephesians 3:2-6, the mystery is explained in terms of its results so that the unity of Jews and Gentiles in the church is the mystery. God's glorious riches are available in Christ (cf. Eph. 1:7, 18; 2:7; 3:8, 16). Such riches are available to Christians because of their confident understanding and full knowledge of Christ.

As Paul prepares to address the teaching that suggests Christ alone is not enough and that supplements are needed, notice his focus. Unity and the richness of God are possible through understanding and full knowledge of Christ. Christ is the totality. Even in this paragraph where Paul is describing his ministry, he includes references to Christ's fullness and completeness as the fulfillment of God's purpose.

2:3-5. "In Christ are hidden all the treasures (*thesauros*) of wisdom and knowledge (*gnosis*)." This statement magnifies Christ and shows that in Christ all knowledge is available to all Christians. Paul writes so the Colossians will not be deceived (*paralogizomai*) by persuasive words (*pithanologia*). The word translated "deceived" includes various deceptions, delusions, or distortions, false reasoning, and even fraud. In this context, Paul warns against philosophical reasoning, argumentation that sounds plausible on the surface, and persuasive words. How amazing it is that false teaching almost always appears logical and attractive. Paul assures them of his presence with them in spirit even though he is physically absent. Epaphras has reported to Paul that the church still has members who maintain orderliness and firmness in the midst of the threat of false teaching.

> *"As you have received Christ Jesus the Lord, keep on living your lives in him, having been firmly rooted in him, being continually built up in him, established in faith as you were taught, overflowing with gratitude."*
>
> Col. 2:6-7

2:6-19. The importance of Paul's references in 2:1-5 is seen by remembering that the problem with false teachers included a mixture of Christianity and Jewish philosophy. Jewish philosophy incorporated concepts from Greek philosophy and Judaism, resulting in a religious and philosophical system that tended to measure success by factors such as legalism, asceticism, and various Jewish traditions and practices. These Paul will now address.

2:6-7. Paul begins with a positive admonition. The Colossians had received the gospel message, and in receiving the message had received (*paralambano*) Christ Jesus the Lord. Having begun with a focus on Christ as Lord, keep living that way. Jesus is Lord, in the sense of being supreme or preeminent, reflecting concepts from Chapter 1. Walk (present imperative, *peripateo*, to live or to conduct your life) in him. Christian faith leads to a Christian lifestyle; the lifestyle of faith is consistent and continuous. The admonition to walk introduces four dependent participial phrases that also have imperatival force: having been firmly rooted (perfect tense participle), being built up in him (present tense), established in faith (present tense) as you were taught, and overflowing (present tense) with gratitude.

2:8-15. These verses are one sentence in Greek, presenting one major idea, and therefore are treated together in these comments and notes.

Paul moves from the positive admonition of vv. 6-7 to words of warning: beware (present active imperative). Christians must be on guard. It is possible to be led away (*sulagogeo*, to lead away as the booty or spoils of conquest, to lead captives, to lead away in the sense of to seduce). In the context, seduce may best communicate the meaning, although false teachers are always seeking followers whom they can captivate, influence and control. The seduction is through philosophy and empty deceit that are according to (*kata*) human traditions.

Paul uses *kata* three times: according to human traditions, not according to Christ, according to the basic principles (*stoicheion*) of the world. Christians must constantly check to make certain their faith is based on the Bible and not on humanly derived understandings that arise over a period of time within a cultural context. Such human reasoning is a step removed from following Christ. The gospel depends on divine revelation and not on human reasoning. *Stoicheon* (plural, *stoicheia*) is something put in order as in a row or series. The word was used to refer to the building blocks of the world (2 Pet. 3:10; these elements were air, water, earth and fire in first century understanding), basic teaching about a subject (cf. Heb. 5:12), basic principles that control children (Gal. 4:3), and basic principles to which the Galatians were being tempted to return (Gal. 4:8-9). Christians have died to the basic elements of the world in Christ (2:20).

Paul is not presenting a complete condemnation of philosophy. Rather, he is warning against a misuse of philosophy that results in deceptive arguments and conclusions. The passage describes Paul's rejection of the philosophical system that was part of the Colossian heresy, "the philosophy that is empty and deceitful."

2:9-10. The reason for rejecting the empty philosophical system is that the fullness of Deity (*theotes*, used only here in the New Testament) dwells in Christ even as he exists in bodily form. The honor or reverence due God as spirit is due to Christ, even though he came to earth in human form. The present tense form of "to dwell" suggests continuity. The deity and humanity of Jesus were not mutually exclusive. The basis of Paul's argument here has already been presented in 1:19-20. Jesus is the fullness (*pleroma*) and you are made full (*pleroo*, to complete) in him. He is head over all powers (1:16; cf. also 2:15 below). No rule or authority exists that can add to Christ.

2:11-15. Two introductory observations about this passage are important. First, Paul uses the Old Testament covenant sign of circumcision in a spiritual sense. This is figurative language. There is no reference to Jewish circumcision in the context, except the disclaimer of v. 11 that Jewish physical circumcision is not what Paul is talking about. The figurative circumcision Paul is describing must be understood by the contextual references. Second, in v. 14, God obliterates or erases the handwritten certificate of indebtedness (an IOU) that was against us, a document that was expressed in legal decrees and demands. He has lifted it out of the midst, nailing it to the cross. In the context, what is this document based on legal requirements that was in the middle? This must be explained keeping in mind the context of the passage. Many traditional interpretations of these verses have focused on Jewish circumcision and the Old Testament nailed to the cross. Paul's subject is the impact Christ has had in the lives of the Colossian believers. Whatever understanding we come to concerning these verses must have an application in the lives of the recipients, an application for both Gentile and Jewish believers in Colossae. If the Colossian church was primarily or almost exclusively Gentile, the traditional interpretation of this passage makes little sense.

The construction of the text is that vv. 11-12 present a thought that is completed by v. 13. Then v. 14 presents a thought that is completed by v. 15. This construction is not maintained in some English versions, resulting in connections and readings that do not exist in the original text.

2:11-13. In vv. 11-12, Paul sets forth the situation of Christians "in him" because of what has been done "by him," because of what they have experienced "with him" and "with him." This statement leads to v. 13: and, you being dead in transgressions and without the circumcision of Christ, he made alive "with him" having forgiven all your transgressions. Christians, having been buried with him in baptism, were raised with him through faith, and are made alive with him. Observe that the focus of these verses is on Christ. In vv. 11-13, the Christian is described in several ways: circumcised figuratively because the body of flesh is removed by the circumcision of Christ, having been buried in baptism, being raised, formerly dead in transgressions and uncircumcision, made alive, having been forgiven.

The circumcision that the Colossian Christians had experienced was a circumcision "made without hands." The typical way of referring to Jewish circumcision was as a circumcision "done with hands." The circumcision Paul is describing is not Jewish circumcision. The circumcision Paul is describing is the removal of the "body of flesh." This does not refer to the literal physical body. The removal of the figurative "fleshly body" makes way for the "spiritual body." This process is described as the "circumcision of Christ." To remove the old fleshly body in favor of a new body may remind us of the destruction of the "body of sin" in baptism (Rom. 6:6). The same process is described in 3:5-11 under the figure of the "old man" and the "new man," using the same verb (*apekduomai*).

2:12. Connected with this circumcision is an action described in a dependent participle: having been buried with him… The "circumcision of Christ" was experienced in the past action of burial (aorist participle) in baptism. The result described in v. 11 was accomplished by the action of v. 12. Baptism is the death of the old person and the birth of the new person. In 2:12-13, believers share with Christ in baptism, in resurrection, and in new life.

You were raised up with him. The result of burial in baptism with Christ is being raised with him. Baptism and resurrection to new life are linked here as in Rom. 6:4-6. To be raised with Christ is through faith in the resurrecting power of God, the same power that raised Jesus from the dead (cf. Eph. 1:19-20).

2:13. This verse completes the thought of vv. 11-12. "You, being dead in transgressions and uncircumcision…" The phrase refers to spiritual death, separation from God. The uncircumcision of this verse refers to a time before the Colossians had experienced the circumcision of Christ (v. 11). Before they experienced the circumcision of Christ, they were dead in sin. The reference is to both Jews and Gentiles. To read this as only referring to the Gentiles misses the point and is too much focused on Jewish circumcision as the subject of the text, which we have shown it is not. Both Jews and Gentiles were dead in transgressions without the circumcision of Christ that removed the "fleshly body." Both were "uncircumcised" in the sense of this passage.

He (God) made you alive with Christ. The subject pronoun of this section through v. 15 is God the Father. Christians are buried-with, raised-with, and quickened-with. Christians participate with Christ in baptism, resurrection, and life. The main verb, made alive, is connected to the participle (having forgiven, *charizomai*) that follows: "made alive, having forgiven all transgressions." God can forgive all sins on the basis of Jesus' death on the cross. All things can be reconciled through the peace that comes by the blood of the cross (1:20-22). Just as the Christians at Colossae were circumcised with the circumcision of Christ, having been buried in baptism, also they were made alive, having received forgiveness. Baptism is the means of the circumcision of Christ that puts off the old body. Forgiveness is the means of life with Christ. It is impossible to have new life without forgiveness. Forgiveness is often seen as the result of the new life in Christ, but here it precedes new life, making new life possible. This understanding is consistent with the teaching of Romans 6. The old person (the body of sin in Rom. 6:6, the fleshly body here) is removed in baptism. There is no new person before baptism. The new life is not possible without forgiveness. Again, forgiveness is not the result of the new life but the means of the new life.

2:14-15. In these verses begins a new sentence, and a new thought. He (God the Father) erased (*exaleipho*, to smear out, to obliterate, to wipe out) what was against us, the handwritten certificate of indebtedness based in legal demands. Not only did God erase it, he lifted it out of the middle, out from the midst. In the first century, this document could be an IOU, a signed confession, or an indictment proving guilt.

Bear with me a short time as we explore what this document is in the context of Colossians 2 and Paul's concern about the false teaching that was being advanced in Colossae. Paul's explanation of the passage must somehow relate to the false teachers. The point Paul makes is that no legal-based requirements can any longer stand between God and the Christian, because God in Christ has removed every possible basis for accusation. First, he erased the document, effectively canceling any legal obligations that could arise from legal demands. Second, he removed it. For the Jews, this could possibly refer to the Mosaic Covenant that stood between God and his people, setting forth the Law and legal requirements that the Jews could not keep. However, the Gentiles were never subject to the Old Testament. The Old Testament was a covenant only between God and Israel, that is, the Jews (Ex. 34:27-28). Since the Gentiles were never subject to the Old Testament, what is the message of this text to them, especially if the reference is limited to the Old Testament? Is this text not true and applicable also for the Gentiles?

One possibility is to say that also for the Gentiles God erased the certificate of their indebtedness that was based on legal demands, the record of their transgressions and obligations before God. The relationship between the Gentiles and God was also blocked by sin, and the record of that sin God erased and removed by attaching it to the cross, where the blood shed was sufficient for peace and reconciliation (1:19-20). For all people in all times, in Christ and the cross, God erased and removed all evidence of indebtedness. In this case, the certificate of debt would be figurative, just as was circumcision in the preceding illustration.

Another possibility is that Paul is addressing attempts to integrate various Old Testament Jewish practices with Christianity, using Jewish philosophical teachings as supplements to Christianity. In this context, the point is that such Old Testament practices cannot be required for either Jew or Gentile because that document and those legal decrees were erased and taken away by God when they were nailed to the cross. In this case, the reference is to the Old Testament, but with a specific application to those at Colossae who were attempting to add certain required practices to Christianity. Christ's death on the cross makes it impossible to impose such demands.

2:15. This verse continues the thought from v. 14 but has its own main verb. The main thought of the sentence is that "God openly exhibited," or, God publicly displayed. The sentence begins with a participial phrase, "having stripped away rulers and authorities." The verb (*apekduomai*, see also 2:11 and 3:9) means to strip away, remove a garment, divest, or renounce. What is the meaning of this phrase in the context? When Christ is above all else, the authorities and powers that were a part of the false philosophy (and were a part of Gnosticism) have no power. God in the cross showed the inadequacy of all other power systems and destroyed spiritual powers that were hostile to humanity (Heb. 2:14 presents a parallel thought, although the specific Greek word is not used there). God declared all other powers powerless, and he put them on public display, having triumphed (*thriambeuo*, to conquer) over them. This description is usually understood as referring to the triumphal parade of a victorious army (cf. 2 Cor. 2:14). God made clear at the cross the sufficiency and supremacy of Christ, and the adequacy of his work to accomplish God's purposes. Nothing else is needed — nothing but Christ!

2:16-19. In 2:16-19 Paul addresses the legalistic requirements that were apparently being added as Jewish philosophy was integrated with Christianity. In 2:20-23, he addresses tendencies toward asceticism. These appear to be two aspects of the false teaching, but the parallel constructions and thoughts in 2:20 and 3:1 suggest making 2:20-23 and 3:1-4 a single thought unit. Regardless of how one chooses to divide the text, careful analysis shows that the frequently used outline of Chapters 1-2 as the doctrinal section and Chapters 3-4 as the practical section is not as clear as some would have us believe.

2:16-17. Do not let anyone judge (*krino*, condemn, criticize) you about food, drink, or in the matter of a feast, new moon, or Sabbaths. These appear to have to do with practices that were being carried over from Judaism. These things are a shadow (*skia*) of what is to come, but the body is of Christ. Since, in the context, body is the antonym of shadow, translations such as reality or substance reflect the meaning better than the literal translation. What matters is Christ. That Paul calls these things the shadow answers exactly to the teaching of the heretics that real substance was to be found in special knowledge and special acts of devotion that would set apart the spiritually elite.

2:18-19. Do not let anyone defraud (*katabrabeuo*, to act as umpire against, to decide against, to rule against) you. This verse is parallel to 2:16: to judge, to rule against. Those against whom Paul is warning are those who delight in humility and worship (*threskeia*, ceremonial observance) of angels. Worship of angels is also carried over from Judaism. Based on the context, humility is often translated as "false humility." When translated as self-abasement, the word foreshadows the asceticism of vv. 20-23 as an evidence of religious devotion. Self-denial has often been seen as a sign of spirituality, a view that is still current today. The opponents are further described as those who depend on what they have seen, becoming proud (*phusioo*, inflated or puffed up) without reason because of their fleshly mind. These descriptions refer to those who claimed to see what others could not see, to have special revelations and special knowledge. They are proud, but their pride comes not from spiritual thinking but from their fleshly minds.

These no longer hold on to (*krateo*) the head. "Head" refers to Christ. The metaphor of head and body was used earlier in the book and refers to Christ and the church. Those who are disconnected from Christ are missing entirely the only true source of strength that supplies, connects, and gives growth to the body.

2:20-23. This section begins a new thought. The phrasing of 2:20 is parallel to 3:1, suggesting that these verses introduce two contrasting sub-sections within a larger literary unit. Colossians presents some unique problems in paragraphing as one looks at sentence structures, conjunctions, and contextual and thematic factors.

2:20-22. "If you have died with Christ…" The first class condition is true, "since" you have died with Christ, or "because" you have died with Christ. Believers are dead to the basic principles (*stoicheion*, cf. 2:8) of the world because of their union with Christ (v. 19). The death mentioned here is specifically with reference to basic principles that guide the thinking of the world. The phrase "with Christ" may build on 2:12-13.

Why do you submit to decrees (same word root as 2:14), as if you were still living according to (*en*, in) the world? Paul mentions three examples of such decrees: do not handle, do not taste, do not touch. These phrases have been frequently quoted out of context, as though they were Bible teaching to be obeyed. In the context, Paul is saying that these decrees are not sufficient guides for the Christian. These are given as examples of human rules. These have to do with perishable things and are based on human commands and teachings.

2:23. The problem with such things, as with much humanly devised teaching, is that they appear to be right, they look wise, and they sound good. Who can be against improving religious practice, having a little more humility, and self-denial? The word, *ethelothreskeia*, appears only here in the

New Testament. The frequent translation is "self-made religion," although the NET "self-imposed worship" also communicates the idea. "Humility" is repeated from 2:18, and again the context suggests false humility or self-abasement. In the context, neglect (*apheidia*) of the body refers to asceticism. The point is that the legalistic and ascetic teachings were not helpful in guarding against the gratification (*plesmone*) of the flesh.

CHAPTER SUMMARY

Paul continues his description of his ministry in the gospel, calling special attention to the assurance, insight, and knowledge available in Christ, in whom is hidden all wisdom and knowledge. Although Paul is not with them, he is present in spirit and concerned about the deceptive arguments they are encountering.

Christ is everything. You received him, you live in him. You are rooted, built up, and firm in him. Be careful that you are not seduced by empty, deceitful philosophy that follows worldly thinking and human traditions and does not follow Christ. Christ is the fullness of Deity, and you are fully complete in him as he rules over everything. Let me illustrate it for you. First, when you were circumcised with the circumcision of Christ (not Jewish circumcision), you saw how powerfully he removed your fleshly person. He did this as you were baptized with him, raised with him, and made alive with him, even though you had formerly been dead in trespasses and without the circumcision of Christ. His ability to forgive despite your past again shows his power. Second, he erased and removed your indebtedness from legal demands, nailing that to the cross. In the cross, he showed how powerless all other powers are, and through the cross he publicly displayed his triumph over all.

Now when anyone wants to apply new legal demands, you know that such is not necessary to prove the power of Christ in your life. Don't put up with requirements about food and drink and various ceremonies. Those are shadow, Christ is the reality. Don't let anyone rule you out, trying to show how much better they are than you on the basis of their humility, worship of angels, special revelation, or false pride that really comes from thinking like the world more than from thinking like Christ. In reality, they are totally disconnected from Christ, and therefore unable to receive God's support, strength, and growth.

Since you have died with Christ to worldly thinking and worldly principles, why do you go on living like they matter? In fact, you are submitting to superficial rules about what you can handle, taste or touch. Don't you see that such things are not eternal and that such ideas are based on human commands and teachings. Oh, they look good, and wise, and right. The truth is that self-made religious rules, hypocritical humility, and self-denial do not really help us deal with the desires of the flesh.

Colossians 3

[Note: it is suggested that the student read the introductory materials on pages 3-8 of this guide before beginning an individual preparatory reading and analysis.]

CONTENT

The paragraphing included in the Content section of each chapter gives suggestions for the work the reader should do for himself. The student is encouraged to identify the paragraphs and subsections within each paragraph to assist in his own study. The division of the biblical text into paragraphs is fairly standard in modern translations.

Outline of the Chapter

3:1-4, dying and living, life with Christ (continuation of paragraph that begins in 2:20)

3:5-17, the old life and the new life (vv. 5-11, vv. 12-17)

3:18-4:1, Christian duties of the new life

Observations about the Content of the Chapter

This chapter is the continuation of an extended literary section that began in 2:20. Four basic sub-units can be identified within the chapter.

In 3:1-4, the phrase "raised with Christ" contrasts with the phrase "died with Christ" in 2:20. The passage in 2:20-3:4 functions as a literary unit within a larger section.

In 3:5-11, the contrast of the old man and the new man points to Christ as everything.

In 3:12-17, instructions for life with Christ together in the body show the importance of including others rather than excluding.

In 3:18-4:1, admonitions about family life show how Christ changes relationships in every part of life.

STUDY HELPS

3:1-4. "If then (*oun*) you have been raised with Christ." The conjunction (*oun*) also appears in 2:6, 2:16, and 3:5. While the conjunction connects thoughts, and can also serve to connect literary sections, it is unlikely that here it serves to connect the first two chapters (doctrinal section) with the last two chapters (practical section). In the context, it is preferable to see its function as connecting 2:20-23 (if you died with Christ) with 3:1-4 (if you have been raised with Christ).

3:1-2. "If" introduces a first class conditional sentence (as in 2:20). "Since you have been raised with Christ, keep seeking (*zeteo*, present active imperative indicates continuous action) things above, where Christ is seated at the right hand of God." To die with Christ separates the believer from the basic elements of the world; to be raised with Christ connects the believer to things above. The two phrases in 2:20 and 3:1 provide several corresponding contrasts. Raised with Christ repeats the wording from 2:12-13. The imperative of v. 2, "think about (*phroneo*) the things above" parallels v. 1 and repeats the words, "things above" (*ta ano*). We are formed by what we seek and think about. The alternative to thinking about things above is to think about things on the earth.

3:3-4. "You have died" repeats the thought of 2:20. The contrast in v. 3 is easily missed. "You died so your life is hidden." That is, you died in order to live. Your life has been hidden (perfect tense) with Christ in God. Note the frequent repetition of the phrase "with him" or "with Christ" throughout the book. Christ is the source of spiritual life, but more is affirmed here. The idea that "Christ is life" has parallels in Phil. 1:21, to live is Christ, and in Gal. 2:20, Christ lives in me. When Christ is revealed, then also you will be revealed with him in glory. The reference is to Christ's coming again.

3:5-11. "Then (*oun*) put to death (aorist active imperative) your members that are of the earth." The primary thrust of this section is that believers are to put off evil in order to put on the new man. The next section (3:12-17) will consider virtues to be included in the believer's life. The list of evils includes fornication, uncleanness, passion, evil desire, and greed. Fornication (*porneia*) includes all kinds of sexual immorality. Impurity (*akatharsia*) means sexual immorality and moral uncleanness. In the context, the second meaning is more likely. Passion (*pathos*) can refer to suffering but here it refers to shameful passion (NET). Desire (*epithumia*) can be toward evil or toward good, but here the first meaning is clear based on context. Greed describes a desire for things. Paul says such desire is idolatry.

Because of these things, the wrath of God comes on the sons of disobedience. A longer list of things that bring God's wrath appears in Rom. 1:18, 29-31.

3:7-11. You once lived *(peripateo*, to walk) in these things, when you were living (*zao*) in them. The first verb refers to conduct, the second means to live. Your conduct was characterized by such things when you were living in (*en*) them. Some have considered these sins so unlikely among the Jews that this statement must surely refer only to the Gentiles. Such a view fails to recognize the composition of the Colossian church where there were undoubtedly both Jewish and Gentile believers. Not every recipient of the letter was participating in all of the sins that are mentioned, nor is this list all-inclusive. Paul's instruction is to put to death the worldly things in your life. In the text are some samples. But do not consider yourself acceptable before God simply because you pass the test with regard to the sins that are mentioned in the text. All worldliness in our lives is to be removed (put to death). "Living in them" may mean "continuing to do them" or may mean "living among them" (cf. 1:27). The former seems to fit the context best.

3:8. But now put aside (aorist imperative) also all of these: anger, rage, malice, slander, and filthy speech. In this verse and several following verses, Paul continues the idea of taking off and putting on garments, a common New Testament metaphor. Put off these things (v. 8), put off the old man (v. 9), put on the new man (v. 10), put on (v. 12).

3:9-11. These verses are one sentence in Greek. Do not lie to one another, since you have (literally, having, an aorist participle describing past action) put aside the old man with its practices. And have (literally, having, another aorist participle) put on the new (the word man is not in the text but is understood) who is being renewed to full knowledge *(epignosis)* according to the image (*eikon*) of the one creating him. The verb is passive, representing God's work in renewal. This renewal makes us more and more like Christ (cf. 1:16, Christ as creator).

3:11. "Where there is not Greek and Jew, circumcised and uncircumcised, barbarian, Scythian, slave, free, but Christ is all and in all." In the process of putting on the new and experiencing the renewal that brings full knowledge of Christ, his nature and his work, there are no distinctions. The barriers that the world honors do not exist in Christ. The application is to salvation in Christ, not to biblical roles and responsibilities. In Christ inequality is removed, which is in contradistinction to the efforts of the false teachers to establish superiority. Barbarian refers to the uncultured; the Scythians were considered especially uncivilized.

3:12-17. This section of positive instructions is often seen as the other side of the mostly negative instructions in vv. 5-11. Paragraphing is difficult; some would begin the new paragraph at v. 9 on the basis of content, but the extended sentence in vv. 9-11 seems sufficient to justify the break between v. 11 and v. 12. As reflected in the chapter outline above, the best option seems to identify vv. 5-17 as a single unit, separated from 2:20-3:4 with the conjunction *oun*. Alternatively, one may see 2:20-3:17 as a unit with subsections in 2:20-23, 3:1-4, 3:5-11, and 3:12-17.

3:12. Paul's description of the church as elect, holy, and loved reflects Old Testament descriptions of Israel that are frequently used by Paul in his letters. "Put on" (aorist imperative) continues the metaphor of donning and taking off garments. This same terminology Paul uses concerning baptism (cf. Gal. 3:27, put on Christ). Just as he did with the evils to be put off, Paul provides a list of characteristics to be put on: tenderheartedness, kindness, humility, gentleness, and patience. Tender-heartedness is literally "bowels of compassion" and is often translated mercy. Kindness governs relationships with others. Christian humility is genuine and not proud (cf. 2:18, 23). Gentleness was used of domesticated animals. Patience addresses our attitude toward others and how we treat others. It is likely that these were largely lacking in the false teachers.

3:13. "Bearing with" (*anechomai*, to forbear, put up with, endure, suffer) one another. The participle form depends on the main verb in v. 12 (put on) and describes how one puts on these characteristics. Put on these characteristics by putting up with one another and by "forgiving one another." The word used here for forgiveness comes from the same root as the Greek word for grace. God's grace enables us to be forgiven by God, to forgive others, and to be forgiven by others. The forgiveness human beings extend to one another is the fruit of God's forgiveness of us. The phrase "if anyone toward any other has a quarrel (*momphe*)" connects to the participles. The third class condition indicates probable future action. Christians will have disagreements, conflicts, quarrels, and complaints. It is precisely in the midst of such situations that it is essential to be forbearing and forgiving. Our model of forgiveness is the Lord himself. We follow his example in forgiveness, just as he forgave us.

3:14. "On top of (*epi*) all of this, put on love which is the bond (*sundesmos*) of completeness (*teleiotes*)." "Put on" is not in the Greek text but is supplied as the continuation of v. 12. My preference for translating "bond of completeness" is "perfect bond."

3:15. "Let the peace of Christ rule (*brabeuo*, to govern) in your hearts, unto which you were called in one body, and be thankful." Christians are called to peace. That peace is to be realized in one body, not in many separate bodies. Based on the context, peace refers to the peace between human beings in interpersonal relationships. An intensified form of the verb "rule" was used in 2:18, referring to the desire of the false teachers to pass judgment on others. The peace of Christ is the lens through which Christians see one another. The present imperative form indicates that gratitude is continuous in the Christian life.

3:16. "(You, plural) let the word of Christ dwell in you richly..." "Word of Christ" is found only here in the New Testament. The reference is likely to the teachings of Christ. The subject matter in 3:12-15 reminds one of Jesus' teaching in the Beatitudes. Whether Christ's teachings dwell within us is our choice. The imperative form tells us that this is God's will and God's instruction for our lives. "In (*en*) you" can be translated "among you." The difference in the emphasis determines whether the instruction is individual or corporate. The plural imperative suggests a corporate application: "All of you should let the word of Christ dwell in your midst." This verse is parallel to Eph. 5:18, where the Christian life is made possible by being filled with the Spirit. Considering the parallel, letting Christ's word dwell in us and being filled with the Spirit may refer to the same thing. Obviously, both empower the Christian life.

The main verb, to dwell, is expanded with a series of dependent participles: teaching, admonishing, singing. The participles are similar to those in Eph. 5:19-21—speaking, singing, making melody, giving thanks, submitting. "With all wisdom" probably goes with "teaching" and "admonishing." Teaching (*didasko*) and admonishing (*noutheteo*, to warn, to call to mind) one another indicates a shared activity, even as the main verb is a plural imperative. Teaching and encouraging are not one-way streets. Every Christian is obligated to every other Christian. The third participle, "singing" is to be done with psalms, hymns and spiritual songs, with grace in your hearts to God. Singing "with grace" contrasts to teaching and admonishing "with wisdom," providing as it were parentheses to open and close the verse.

This verse mentions three ways we let the Word of Christ dwell in us: by teaching one another, by admonishing one another, and by singing to God. The first two participles are immediately followed by "to one another." The last participle is followed by "to God." Different types of songs are mentioned—psalms, hymns, and spiritual songs. It appears that all were known and were being sung in the early church. The last participle in this verse is specific—singing! The music Paul describes in this verse is singing. Whether "in psalms, hymns, and spiritual songs" modifies only the participle "singing," or whether the phrase also modifies teaching and admonishing is not clear. The same list of musical types in Eph. 5:19 is connected to the participle "speaking to one another." The speaking of Eph. 5:19 most likely refers to singing, based on the parallel. If "teaching and admonishing" are controlled by the list of musical types in this verse, these actions were also done by singing.

3:17. Every word and every action of a Christian is in the name of, by the authority of, the Lord Jesus, and is done with gratitude that is extended to God the Father through Him (Jesus). This verse summarizes. Jesus is supreme. Jesus is Lord. Jesus has all authority. Nothing needs to be added to Jesus. Every aspect of the Christian life is measured by the word of Christ.

3:18-4:1. In the literature of the first century, it was common to enumerate the mutual responsibilities among members of a household, including slaves. In this section of the Colossian letter, Paul writes about the home from a Christian viewpoint and presents the mutual relationship between wives and husbands, between children and parents, and in even greater detail, the relationship between slaves and masters. The parallel passage in Ephesians is found in 5:22-6:9. Such instructions are often seen in a negative light today, but in the first century, they were considered important and helpful. The focus is on the mutuality of these relationships within the home and family.

3:18-19. "Wives, be subject (*hupotasso*) to your husbands as is proper in the Lord." In this passage, as in Ephesians, the one who in the cultural context was thought of as weaker is considered first, but all are instructed equally, including those who had power in the cultural context. "As is proper" simply means that this is the right thing to do as a Christian.

The subjection described in this passage, as in other New Testament passages, is between a wife and her husband, not in the relationships of men and women generally. The parallel text in Ephesians makes clear that submission applies to everyone. Eph. 5:21 teaches mutual submission for all Christians. Jesus himself submitted to the Father, and every Christian submits to God and to Jesus as Lord. In our day of personal rights, submission is rejected. Even subjection to authority and governments is questioned. Submission goes against the individualism of our Western worldview. It is, however, a valid biblical principle that has application in the life of every person.

"Husbands, love your wives, and do not bitter toward them." A bitter attitude often results in harsh treatment. Husbands are to treat their wives right.

3:20-21. Children are to be obedient (present active imperative signifies continuous action). "Always keep on being obedient." Again, a concluding phrase notes that this is the right thing to do: this is well-pleasing to the Lord.

"Fathers, do not provoke (*erethizo*, to cause to be resentful or angry) your children." Children who experience constant tension with their parents will become disheartened (*athumeo*, to be dismayed).

3:22-4:1. "Slaves, obey in all things you earthly masters." "Obey in all things" is a way of saying "obey completely" and does not extend to disobedience to God's will. The obedience that slaves owe their masters comes from a sincere (*haplotes*, without hypocrisy, not self-seeking) heart and the fear of the Lord. It is not based on whether the master is watching or not. Christian slaves were different from those slaves who were "people-pleasers."

The instructions to slaves continue in vv. 23-25, although the principles can easily be applied to every Christian. Whatever work we do is done for the Lord; Christians are always servants of the Lord first. We serve others because we are servants of the Lord Christ. This attitude causes the Christian to work with enthusiasm. The reward that we seek comes from the Lord, not from men. The reference to an inheritance in v. 24 was especially significant in the first century where slaves had no inheritance. A general principle that can be observed in all activities is this: one who does wrong will receive according to what he does wrong. This is true of both human reward and divine reward.

4:1. This verse belongs with the paragraph that began in 3:18, as it continues to treat the slave-master relationship. It appears that the masters being addressed are Christians who were slave owners. "Masters, give (*parecho*) justice and fairness to your slaves." The reason given for the action is that the masters also have a heavenly master. Even in the slave-master relationship, mutuality and reciprocity are desirable, especially for Christians. It is often observed that the modern parallel to the slave-master relationship may be in the employee-employer relationship. Remember that this letter was sent at the same time the letter to Philemon was sent, and that Onesimus, a runaway slave, was accompanying Tychicus as he carried the letters from Paul to Colossae.

CHAPTER SUMMARY

Because you have died with Christ to the things of the world, you are not obligated to follow traditions and human expectations that are based on worldly thinking. You can look around and see that such thinking looks good but does not improve morality. (2:20-23)

Because you have been raised with Christ, look at heavenly things, remember that you have died to earthly things, and look forward to authentic and glorious life in Christ. This will all be clear when he comes again.

Since you have died with Christ, put to death all of the things that belong to this world. These bring God's wrath. You remember that you used to participate in them, but now you have put off the old and all such actions and have put on the new that changes what you know and changes your very nature. All of this is possible because Christ is everything—in all, through all, for all.

Because you are God's elect, holy and loved by him, put on Christlikeness. That includes forgiveness, love, and peace. You can do this by putting Christ's word in your lives, in the wisdom of your teaching and encouraging one another, and in the grace of your singing to God. This is not a complete list of actions, so follow this principle. Whatever you do in words or actions, do it to the Lord Jesus. When you think of how he has changed your life, how can you not give thanks to God through Jesus!

Note: 3:18-4:1 are not included in the chapter summary.

Colossians 4

[Note: it is suggested that the student read the introductory materials on pages 3-8 of this guide before beginning an individual preparatory reading and analysis.]

CONTENT

The paragraphing included in the Content section of each chapter is merely a suggestion. The student is encouraged to identify the paragraphs, and subsections within each paragraph, to assist in her own study. The division of the biblical text into paragraphs is usually fairly standard in modern translations.

Outline of the Chapter

3:18-4:1, Christian duties
4:2-6, instructions and exhortations
4:7-15, final greetings
4:16-18, closing

STUDY HELPS

4:1. Comments on this verse are included in the Study Helps for Chapter 3.

4:2-6. The Colossian letter closes somewhat abruptly. This final section before the personal greetings and customary close is quite brief.

    4:2-4. The instructions of this section are related to prayer and the advance of God's message about Jesus Christ. Be diligent (present active imperative, *proskatereo*, persevere, continue) in prayer, being vigilant (*gregoreuo*, awake, watchful) with thanksgiving. The dependent participle functions also as an imperative. Persistence and vigilance in prayer are crucial and Paul repeats himself. "Be diligent in prayer, praying...." Paul asks the Colossians to pray for him and those with him. He asks for their prayers for three things: an open door for the word, to proclaim the mystery, to make it clear. The message is "the word" and "the mystery." Paul understood his obligation to preach the message of Christ and asked for the participation of the Colossians in prayer.

4:5-6. The advance of the message is made easier when Christians live in a way that is consistent with the message. Paul mentions behavior and speech. Walk (present active imperative, *peripateo*, metaphorically, to live) with wisdom toward outsiders, making the most (*exagorazo*, literally to buy up or to redeem, cf. Eph. 5:16) of the time (the opportunity). This admonition makes every Christian intentional in seeking opportunities for the gospel.

Christian speech is with grace and seasoned with salt. In modern language, salty speech often refers to vulgar speech, but in this verse the word is used in a positive sense. Here is a reminder that Christians are the salt of the earth. Christians who heed these instructions will be ready to respond when the opportunities come.

4:7-15. As is Paul's custom, he mentions several of his fellow workers by name in the closing greeting.

4:7-8. Tychicus apparently carried this letter (and the letter to Philemon). He is mentioned in Acts 20:4, Eph. 6:21, 2 Tim. 4:12, and Tit. 3:12. Tychicus would share information concerning Paul's situation in order to comfort (*parakaleo*, also translated to encourage and to exhort) the hearts of the Colossians.

4:9. Onesimus was a runaway slave whose master, Philemon, lived in Colossae. The two letters (Colossians and Philemon) were delivered at the same time. Tychicus and Onesimus were together given the responsibility to explain the situation of Paul in prison.

4:10-14. Six co-workers send greetings: Aristarchus, Mark, Justus, Epaphras, Luke, Demas. The same list of co-workers appears in Philemon, excluding Justus. Aristarchus is described as a fellow prisoner—either literally or metaphorically. Mark is John Mark (see Acts 13:5; 15:36-39). Paul notes that the number of Jews who have stayed with him as fellow workers in the kingdom is limited. They were a comfort (*paregoria*) to Paul. The inclusion of this phrase at the end of v. 11 likely suggests that those mentioned in vv. 12-14 were Gentiles.

Epaphras (1:7) had preached the gospel in Colossae. He was a prayer warrior on behalf of the Colossians. He was also connected to the churches in Laodicea and Hierapolis. Luke was Paul's missionary companion and author of the New Testament books of Luke and Acts. A Christian named Demas would later desert Paul (2 Tim. 4:10).

4:15. Paul sends greetings to those in Laodicea, anticipating his request that the letter be read to the church there also (v. 16). The name Nympha is masculine or feminine based on the accent. (Accents were not included in the original text.)

4:16-18. The letter to the Colossians is to be read in Laodicea, and Paul's letter that was read in Laodicea (a letter now lost, unless it is the letter of Ephesians as some have theorized) is to be read in Colossae. Archippus is also mentioned in Philemon 2 and was apparently a leader in the church in Colossae. The admonition concerning Archippus indicates that he was one of the leaders who had remained faithful in the face of the false teachers.

Paul often wrote a final greeting with his own hand (2 Thess. 3:17) as a mark of genuineness. He likely employed a scribe (amanuensis) to write the letters. "You" is plural. Grace be with all of you.

CHAPTER SUMMARY

To conclude, be vigilant in prayer with gratitude. Pray for me in my preaching, for open doors, for opportunities to proclaim, for clarity. Use the message to control your lives and your speech so that you will be able to use every opportunity to explain the gospel.

I am sending Tychicus and Onesimus to tell you about my situation. Lots of others here also send greetings. Greet those in Laodicea, especially the church in Nympha's house. Share this letter with Laodicea and read the letter they have. Encourage Archippus to finish his ministry. Grace be with all of you.

Introduction to Philemon

The little letter from Paul to his friend Philemon has a unique place in the New Testament. Philemon is a personal letter, the shortest Pauline letter in the New Testament. It is an example of a what a private letter was like in the first century world. It probably fit on a single papyrus sheet. It is identified as a letter to Philemon, although there are also references to Apphia and Archippus and the house church (v. 2) as possible recipients. The content of the letter suggests that Philemon was the primary recipient.

The letter reveals the pastoral heart of the Apostle Paul and provides a helpful model for resolving pastoral conflicts. The methods used by Paul are worthy of imitation. The letter also suggests how Christianity was impacting the social structures of the Roman world as churches were composed of those from different social and economic classes (for example, see the references in Gal. 3:28; Col. 3:11).

Author

The personal nature of the letter convinces most readers that the author was Paul. The books of Colossians and Philemon are closely related as they were sent to the same location. They have the same author, they mention many of the same people, and the greetings and closings are similar. Tychicus carried the letter to the Colossians and traveled with Onesimus (cf. Col. 4:7,9).

Date and Place of Writing

Paul was in prison three times: in Caesarea, in Philippi, and in Rome. Some have seen the possibility of an imprisonment in Ephesus in the texts of 1 Cor. 15:32 and 2 Cor. 1:8. I date this letter, and the other Prison Epistles, during an imprisonment in Rome in the early 60s, as this date best fits the Acts timeline.

Purpose

The letters of the New Testament have unique purposes because they are occasional literature, that is, they were written to specific persons at specific times to address specific circumstances or needs.

The occasion for the letter to Philemon can be understood from the content of the letter. It is helpful to identify some of the people mentioned in the letter and to note what the Bible says about them (comparing the books of Philemon, Ephesians, and Colossians).

- Philemon was a Christian who lived in Colossae. He was the owner of a slave named Onesimus. He was probably a convert of Paul (v. 19), possibly during the three years of Paul's stay in Ephesus (Acts 19).
- Onesimus was a runaway slave of Philemon. He was also a convert of Paul, probably during the time of Paul's imprisonment at Rome (A.D. 61-63). It is uncertain how Paul and Onesimus met. It is commonly thought that both were prisoners, although it has also been suggested that Onesimus was sent on an errand to Paul, or that he sought out Paul after arriving in Rome as a runaway.
- Epaphras was a believer from Asia Minor. He brought word to Paul in prison about the heresy in Colossae and about Philemon's faithfulness.
- Tychicus carried three of Paul's letters: Colossians, Ephesians, and Philemon (Col. 4:7-9; Eph. 6:21-22). It appears that as Onesimus went back to face his master (Philm. 11), he was accompanied by Tychicus.

The immediate purpose of the letter was to encourage Philemon to accept Onesimus back as a slave and also as a brother in Christ.

Lessons

Several lessons can be gleaned from the letter: (1) it shows how Paul did not use his apostolic authority, even though it was available to him, (2) it shows how Paul addressed a specific pastoral situation, (3) it reveals the pastoral heart of Paul, (4) it shows how slaves and slave owners, rich and poor existed together in the churches of the first century, and (5) it tells us that Paul believed he would be released from his imprisonment and would be able to visit Asia Minor again.

Background Information

Exactly how Onesimus came to be a part of the life of Paul during Paul's imprisonment in Rome is not revealed. Once Onesimus made the decision to be a Christian, Paul felt compelled to help him and protect him. The situation of Onesimus was quite tenuous considering the laws of the first century. As a runaway slave, he was considered derelict legally, and the laws allowed punishment to be quite severe, even to the point of death.

The text does not say why he had run away, but once Onesimus became a Christian, he was bound to try to return to his master, regardless of what difficult circumstances he might encounter.

Philemon

[Note: it is suggested that the student read the introductory materials on pages 3-8 of this guide before beginning an individual preparatory reading and analysis.]

CONTENT
The paragraphing included in the Content section of each chapter only gives suggestions and guidance. The student is encouraged to identify the paragraphs, and subsections within each paragraph, to assist in his or her own study. The division of the biblical text into paragraphs is usually fairly standard in modern translations.

Outline of the Chapter
1-3, greeting, salutation
4-7, thanksgiving and commendation for Philemon's love and faith
8-16, Paul makes his appeal on behalf of Onesimus
17-21, Paul encourages Philemon's positive response
22, personal request
23-25, final greetings

STUDY HELPS
1-3. Paul is identified as the author. He also identifies himself as a prisoner (literally, one in bonds) of Christ Jesus, probably a reference to his physical imprisonment, but possibly a spiritual reference to his status as a slave or bondservant of Christ, thus identifying himself with the slave and prisoner Onesimus. It is interesting that he does not identify himself as an apostle, but perhaps not surprising in a personal letter. Timothy is included in the salutation. This refers to Timothy's presence with Paul and that Timothy may be sending greetings. The inclusion of Timothy does not make him a co-author. Some studies have noted that Jesus is described in several different ways in this short letter.

The typical salutation in the Greek letter form included the recipients. Here are mentioned not only Philemon, but also Apphia, Archippus, and a house church in Colossae (which may have met in Philemon's house). The content of the letter seems to indicate that Paul knew Philemon personally, and had perhaps been involved in his conversion to Christ. Grace and peace conclude the salutation in typical fashion.

4-7. Paul's mention of his prayers is common. The Greek letter form often included a salutation (from whom and to whom), a blessing or thanksgiving, a prayer (to the gods, but in biblical literature a prayer to God), and a theme statement.

5. It is not absolutely certain whether Paul had ever visited Colossae. On the basis of internal references in the Colossians letter, it appears that he had not. This conclusion is supported by his statement "I hear of your love and faith." The exact connection between faith and love and the Lord Jesus and the saints is not clear. The text speaks of faith and love toward (*pros*) the Lord and unto (*eis*) all the saints.

6-7. Grammatically, this verse appears to mention the specific content of the prayers in v. 4. (The repeated reference to prayer that appears in some translations is not in the original text.) Paul's prayer for the recipients is that the fellowship of faith (shared faith, or sharing faith) may be effective in or with the knowledge of every good thing which they have in Christ Jesus, so they will continue to bless others as they have blessed Paul and other Christians. Some have seen a reference to evangelism in v. 6.

Brother is singular, indicating that much of the letter will be directed specifically to Philemon.

8-16. This section is Paul's appeal to Philemon on behalf of Onesimus, a request that Philemon accept Onesimus back. Paul motivates Philemon's response by mentioning multiple factors: doing what is right, Paul's authority as an apostle, Paul's age, Paul's imprisonment, Paul's ministry in the conversion of Onesimus, Onesimus's ministry to Paul, Paul's love for Onesimus, Onesimus's changed life, Onesimus's possible ministry to Philemon, Philemon's relationship with Paul, Philemon's salvation, and Philemon's ministry to Paul (the last three from vv. 17-20).

8. Paul could use his apostolic authority and issue an order, but he is confident that Philemon will want to do what is proper (what should be done).

9. Paul refers to himself as an old man and also as a prisoner of Christ Jesus (see comments on prisoner in vv. 1-3).

10-11. Onesimus is identified as Paul's child (*teknon*, often translated as son) spiritually. The name Onesimus means useful or profitable. The literal reading of v. 10 puts the name Onesimus in the last position: I exhort you concerning my son whom I bore in my bonds—Onesimus. Paul says that Onesimus was formerly useless (*achrēstos*), but is now "useful" (*euchrētos* cf. 2 Tim. 4:11) to both Paul and Philemon.

12. Paul uses a legal phrase that can mean "to refer a case to someone." In the first century, the slave owner had many legal rights, including the right of sentencing in the case of a runaway slave (see "Background Information" in the Introduction). Paul mentions how much he cares for Onesimus, how much he cares for Philemon, and his concern for the restoration of relationship between the two.

13-14. Paul would have liked to keep Onesimus with him, and that would have been advantageous for Paul. But Philemon had first rights to his slave. Paul was always very careful not to take advantage of his converts. This is especially true with regard to receiving financial help from the churches he established. The same principle is at work here in his relationship with Philemon. Paul wanted Philemon to know the blessing of love and generosity more than the satisfaction of obedience. The obedient heart is blessed by God; the generous heart is doubly blessed.

15-16. Paul reminds Philemon that all of these events are working for the good. It was not right for Onesimus to flee, but the separation can result in a more stable and continuing relationship in the future since Onesimus will be both a slave and a brother in Christ.

17-21. In this section, Paul continues his appeal but mentions several specific aspects of his personal relationship with Philemon in order to encourage a positive response to the request.

17-18. The two conditional clauses are both true from the author's perspective. Paul and Philemon were sharers together, Onesimus had wronged Philemon. *Koinonos* (v. 17) comes from the same root as *koinonia,* which sometimes has a financial aspect (Phil. 4:15), so this may be a subtle wordplay. Paul would know that his relationship with Philemon was firm when Philemon accepted Onesimus, even as we show love for God by loving those whom God loves, that is, by loving one another. Paul is willing to pay any debt Onesimus owes to Philemon.

19. Paul often used scribes (amanuenses) to write his letters, but here he writes with his own hand (cf. 1 Cor. 16:21; Gal. 6:11; Col. 4:18; 2 Thess. 3:17; Philm. 1:19). The verse continues the thought from vv. 17-18 regarding Paul's willingness to pay the debt. The latter part of the verse is often understood to mean that Paul had been instrumental in converting Philemon to Christianity.

20-21. Note the repetition of the thought of vv. 6-7, refreshing the heart. We can encourage one another by our way of life, and by being sensitive to the needs and desires of others. Paul tactfully communicates his confidence in Philemon's positive response.

22-25. The final section contains a personal request and concluding greetings.

22. Paul expected to be released and to be able to visit Philemon again in Colossae. He believed in the power of the prayers of those who were praying for him.

23-25. The final verses are similar to the conclusion of Colossians. Other Bible study resources give good background studies of the people mentioned here, all of whom were apparently with Paul. The concluding blessing is typical of Paul. "Your" is plural, "spirit" is likely used to indicate the spirit of a person (the self), an idiomatic way of saying "with your selves," also affirming that human beings are spirit beings.

SUMMARY OF THE BOOK
To Philemon, my coworker whom I love, along with others in the church there: grace and peace.

First, I am grateful for the loving faithful influence you have had on the Christians, and I pray that you will have more and more opportunities to share your faith, and that such efforts will continue to be effective, so that people fully know Christ. Your example in these things has been for me a source of joy, not to mention that others have been encouraged.

Now, I want to present to you a special appeal for Onesimus. (I do not want to obligate you by telling you what you should do.) Onesimus has become a Christian. He used to be useless, but now he is very useful to me and I would be helped by his presence here, but I am sending him back to you. You have to decide what to do, but it seems God was at work, so that he was separated from you for a time so you could have him forever, not only as a slave but also as a spiritual brother in the Lord.

I encourage you to receive him as you would receive a Christian brother, as you would receive me. If he owes you money, don't worry about that; I will repay it in full. We all have obligations to one another, and in a sense, you owe me your very self. I know I am asking something from you in the Lord, continue to refresh my spirit by your positive response.

I am confident you will do what is right. Make sure my guest room is ready as I hope to come soon, by your prayers and God's grace. Several send their greetings. Grace be with you all.